The Tiny House Collection
Three Best-Selling Tiny House Books

By J.R. Shepherd

© 2014

All rights reserved. No part of this publication may be reproduced, distributed, or transmitted in any form or by any means, including photocopying, recording, or other electronic or mechanical methods, without the prior written permission of the publisher, except in the case of brief quotations embodied in critical reviews and certain other noncommercial uses permitted by copyright law.

And above all – Enjoy!

Live Small and Be Happy!

Have you ever wondered what it would be like to live in a tiny home? Dream of having a smaller mortgage? Or none at all? Care about living "Green"? Want to live a bit more simply and focus on the things that are really important in life? Then a Tiny House might be the perfect solution for you!

This collection of 3 best-selling books explores Tiny Houses and the lifestyle that comes along with them. It will give you an idea of whether a Tiny House makes sense for you and your family and helps you transition to the idea of living large in a small space.

Inside **The Tiny House Collection** you'll learn:
- Who Tiny Houses are a best fit for
- How Tiny Houses help you slim down your unneeded possessions and focus on the things that are really important to you
- Design and Decorating tips to help you make the most out of your Tiny House space
- The Physical and Emotional benefits of adopting the Tiny House lifestyle
- And much, much more!

Tiny Houses are about focusing on what matters most to you - relationships, hobbies, work, nature, or community. It's never too late to change your focus, and **The Tiny House Collection** will help you get there!

*****

Sign up for J.R.'s Mailing List to be notified of **New Releases** and **Special Sales**: http://eepurl.com/XxKR5

Tiny Houses: A Beginner's Guide to Living Small

Have you ever wondered what it would be like to live in a tiny home? Dream of having a smaller mortgage? Or none at all? Want to live a bit more simply and focus on the things that are really important in life? Tiny houses are becoming more and more achievable for thousands of people all over the world. This is a budding phenomenon that is seriously being considered by many people and for good reasons!

There are many different motivations for adopting a tiny home and the lifestyle that comes with it. Less stress, more money in your pocket, more time to focus on other interests. Of course, people still have many questions about tiny homes. How can I build one? How can I buy one? Does it work for a family, or only for single people? Are the houses still good quality? Most of those questions can easily be answered.

Tiny homes are typically constructed quite well, with good quality materials, and are very durable – they are built for the long haul and people who own them have the expectation that since their home is of good quality, the cost for maintenance and repairs will be minimal. Of course a tiny home makes good monetary sense even before the minimal costs of repairs and maintenance are considered.

Ways that a tiny home will save you money can include less overall cost for a high quality structure that can be built to your specifications and to your individual and particular life style. What is important to you? You will have the ability to make your home meet the demands for how you live and spaces that are more important to you can be emphasized and those that mean less can be deemphasized. Love cooking but don't need a huge television/entertainment room? Make the kitchen the focus of your tiny home! Love outdoor living and spending your time on the porch? Build a bigger porch with your tiny home that acts as an extension of the living space!

You can save on energy costs, water and waste costs, repairs and maintenance, taxes, insurance, mortgage interest, the cost of the land it is on, the overall cost of the original home and so many other things. All of the saved expenses add up quickly, and you'll soon find yourself with much more money than you would have if you lived in a traditional home.

The health benefits tally up rather quickly too. First, saving money offers peace of mind. Most families worry about their finances most every month, but with a tiny home you won't need to. A tiny home takes less time to clean. What kind of things would you spend your time doing if you did not have to clean so much? A tiny home tends to be greener, which in turn benefits our earth. A tiny home makes their owners focus on more important things in life than struggling to pay a mortgage, keep thousands of square feet of a house clean and heated and filled with electricity-draining devices.

Yes, if you have a tiny home you will have fewer things but the things you do own will have more value to you. How many things do you own that you never use? How many things in your house do you have that you don't even like or enjoy? Owning a tiny home is a good reason to de-clutter, both from physical things and from the emotional attachments that go hand-in-hand with them.

A tiny home is an opportunity to redecorate (or decorate) in styles and colors that you appreciate and enjoy. You can add lavish details to the inside and outside of your home to make it cozy and comfortable while still using the space to its best advantage. Many people worry about the size of living in a tiny home, but there are ways to overcome this and make the diminutive space seem much larger. Often these details can easily be incorporated in your decorating strategies.

Tiny home livers are masters at repurposing spaces. Folding tables, chairs, lofts and even dual-purpose beds can make the space feel and seem much larger than it is. Choosing comfortable but quality furniture that is suited to the space and your desires will make most rooms appear larger. These homes can be built with hidden storage spaces and with built-in storage spaces like bookshelves, space for dishes and a pantry, or many other useful things.

Planning your tiny home can be an exhilarating experience, as can living in one. Yes, you have to think and be a bit creative, but imagine getting just what you want in your home – nothing more, nothing less. Imagine the good feelings you will experience by having more financial freedom and more time to do what is important to you.

Many people suffer from their large home ownership. They slave and work to pay for their home and they lose focus on what is important. Parents work to keep up the home and have little time for each other or their families. Some people are owned more by their homes - the high cost of owning a large home, and the time and work that goes into maintaining that home, make a large home become more of a burden than it is worth.

There is another growing trend of tiny home communities. These communities offer friendship and companionship based on common tiny home ownership. For many, this is a plus that offers hope and community. Tiny home owners typically share a lot of the same values and ideas, and tiny home communities are springing up all over the world, based on these shared attributes.

Tiny homes are appealing to many groups. For newlyweds, it offers an opportunity to own a place of their own at a time when many newlyweds don't have that ability. Single people and retired couples are also drawn to tiny home ownership because of lower costs and maintenance, but the peace of mind that comes with fewer things can also be a blessing. Tiny home ownership offers a new start and hope for many. Tiny homes are a way to stamp out homelessness and to give individuals who may not otherwise have a chance to own their own home to do so. Tiny homes offer change and choices – sometimes where there are no other choices, so they can offer hope too. But often they can be the prime choice by simply offering a better alternative to everything else that is out there.

There are many good and motivating reasons to choose a tiny home. They are economical, green, healthy, comfortable, convenient, sturdy, fun, and are quickly becoming the best choice for many people. Tiny homes provide a viable living solution to many sectors of people and they are becoming more and more popular with many groups of people. Tiny homes can be a wise, happy, and comfortable choice for you and your family.

So what, exactly, *is* a tiny home? Tiny homes are typically described as any full-featured, smaller home from about 350 square feet up to about 1,000 square feet. They are sometimes built on trailers or hitches, to make them more mobile. They can also be built on traditional foundations or plots of land, to make them into a more permanent structure.

The square footage definition typically used for a tiny home is relative. We are defining a "tiny" home to be from 300 to 1,000 square feet. A "small" home we define from 1,000 to 2,000 square feet. Now, we are not going to draw a chalk line and say 1,100 square feet is NOT a tiny home – size truly varies depending on our individual perspectives. Let's not get stuck on "the square footage of my house is smaller than your house." Tiny homes mean different things to different people, but they all share the idea of downsizing and living in a simpler environment.

Living in a tiny home can truly feel like a completely different experience because you set your perception levels differently. You notice smaller things. Your intuition and senses pick up changes easier, especially in the subtle energies. The faintest of smells are more noticeable. There is a totally different ambiance in, and around, a tiny home than there is in a McMansion house.

Can we define the feelings of living in a tiny home full-time? Let's try. To start with, you get a feeling of being closer to nature. Not as close as camping in a tent, but certainly closer than in a full size house. The elements are more intimate to your personal environment. Sometimes it is like being in a small boat on the ocean. The waxing and waning of energy currents help you feel the rhythms of life, the heartbeat of nature.

Having a very compact kitchen makes it efficient to cook and prepare meals. You don't have to take many steps to do any task. Often you just turn around. An eat-in kitchen is much easier and more efficient to care for than a dining room separate from the kitchen. Haven't you noticed that people always seem to migrate to and gather in the kitchen anyways? It's the nourishing station of our lives.

Imagine that your entire house can be vacuumed with the cord plugged into one central outlet. A few minutes each day is more than enough to clean house. You might even leave the vacuum plugged in, sitting, waiting for action.

There is also a feeling of confidence you can have when not surrounded by too many things. It is Zen-like. Uncluttered. Easier to manage. When there are too many things, you get a closed-in claustrophobic feeling even in the largest of rooms. Tiny homes have a way of focusing on clutter and disorganization, and forcing us to reorder our lives to revolve around the few things that are most important to us, versus the many things that clutter our space and our minds.

Living in small places brings a forced focus on what is important in life and what isn't. This includes time for friends, studying topics that interest you, or even community service - wherever your desires and interests might lead you. Let's face it: larger homes can be distracting, just by the sheer volume of things that need to be done. So much so that you can be held back from doing and being what is really important in your life.

So, how do you make a tiny house a home? You do it through architectural detail, very efficient use of space, and the personal touches that put art and craftsmanship back into the building of a home. You minimize transitional spaces like hallways and stairwells and increase transition zones to the outdoors. You maximize the use of storage areas with organization and vertical storage. You create an environment that is not just expensive heated storage for stuff, but an environment that supports you, your interests, and your lifestyle. You build a house that's not just a huge, cavernous, soul-less shelter – it's your home.

Who Could Use a Tiny House?

People dream of having big, palatial homes but is it really something that is good for them? In today's economy, tiny homes are not just an option for singles or couples but for families too. Let's take a look at how living in a tiny home can actually be better for different groups of people.

The obvious advantage is that a tiny house is more economical and, in this day and age, this is a big factor to consider for many people. Moving out of a rented house and into your own smaller home becomes a distinct possibility with the reduced costs associated with tiny houses. Then, once you move in, living in a tiny home simplifies your life in more ways than you might initially realize. You no longer have room for clutter and unnecessary things. Every inch of space in your home counts. Everything has a purpose. Another big advantage is that the work needed to maintain and keep your house clean reduces in volume quite a bit too. A tiny home is also more energy efficient, as it takes less energy to cool it or keep it warm.

Benefits to the family members themselves are plenty. Tiny homes are great for family bonding. Big houses tend to have family members cooped up in his/her space and not interacting with the other members of the house. This is not possible in a tiny home. Arguments are resolved fast because you are working and living very closely. Family members learn to live with each other and accept each other's good and bad points.

Of course, it is not possible to have kids cramped inside a tiny home all day. Every child (and even adult) needs his/her outside time. Tiny homes may or may not have large backyards, but there are sure to be fields or gardens to play in nearby. Maybe people who plan and build their own tiny house make sure to include a porch or deck, as this outdoor space often flows seamlessly from the inside and makes the house feel much larger.

There are many ways to make effective use of the space available in a tiny home. Having a lot of shelves in the kitchen for storage is a must, but even these can be designed for dual purposes and to take up the least amount of space. And if you would like to promote the habit of reading books among your children or you just love reading yourself, there are many options for you. It can be a good idea to have a bookshelf spanning an entire wall or to have a built-in reading nook or loft. Use light fixtures on the walls to avoid bulky lamps taking up space. Bunk beds for the children are a great way to save up on space and the children love them too. Sofa beds can be used in the sitting room to have an extra bed for a guest. Use the space under the stairs for storage and beautify your home by adding decorations on top of the storage spaces.

With so many benefits and ideas for utilizing space effectively, who could resist moving into a tiny home? Now that the benefits are coming to light, more and more families are shifting to smaller homes and loving the experience.

Below are some more of the different types of people who may be most interested in tiny houses and a bit more detail about how these homes can work for them specifically.

Downsizers

This group is huge and includes almost everyone whose main motivation in moving into a tiny house is seeking a simpler life. Downsizers are folks shedding and discarding "things" and "stuff" that either no longer serves them or for which they no longer place the same importance on. They are cleaning out closets and sorting through items in basements, attics and garages. They are recycling their unused and unwanted possessions through fundraisers such as Goodwill, Habitat for Humanity, church and hospital consignment shops, yard sales, moving sales, the classifieds and dumpsters. If you prefer to give your unwanted items directly to people who can use them, then try freecycle.org, a web site established specifically to help people help each other directly.

In ancient times, tithing referred to leaving part of the harvest to go back into and replenish the soil. It also referred to saving 10% of the seeds for next year's planting. Today, tithing literally means giving money, or in-kind contributions, to charitable purposes. Tithing is one good way to downsize with a purpose.

There are many forms of tithing. Clothes tithing, tool tithing, furniture and art tithing. Adding the concept of tithing to giveaways lends a service component and intrinsic value to an item because someone can use it. This takes more effort and conscious intent than just dumping stuff in the dumpster and filling up our landfills. It is far more rewarding to help others and honor the value of an item that is still usable.

Downsizing includes folks whose life patterns have changed through unemployment, death, separation or divorce, re-treading for a different career or to get more education, retirement, or new life patterns and directions. Shedding old stuff and old ways often opens the door for a new and expanded life to begin. Beginning this new phase of life makes perfect sense in a tiny home.

Empty Nesters

Kids grow up and leave. That's what they are supposed to do, right? That means more bedrooms and baths than the parents need. As life changes, so do housing needs. As people start looking around at all the rooms, storage, and stuff in their empty nest, they begin to realize that they could easily live, and thrive, with much less space. The time it takes to clean those empty bedrooms and rarely used *things* could be used for other fun activities. And then there are the heating and cooling bills that must be paid, possibly out of a fixed income or retirement income. The prospect of a smaller, cozy home becomes increasingly in the forefront while pondering the next phase of life. For many couples or single people at this stage of their lives, a tiny home makes all the sense in the world.

Nest Returners

Do you have that special child that won't, or can't, leave the nest — or keeps coming back, and back, and back home? Are all of your kids nicknamed "boomerang"? Life situations change; sometimes family members need a place to land — having a separate place for them to land (like a detached tiny home in the backyard) might make everyone's life easier.

Pre-Retirement & Retirees

You've worked hard all your life and now it's time to step down. You may be taking some well deserved time off or changing careers or moving to a new location entirely. The best part is yet to come. With the educational opportunities and web-based training that is available, many people are having multiple careers. Why not "retire early and often"?

Life is too precious to spend in a job or career you are not passionate about. And, let's face it, once you have done something for an extended period of time, you may grow tired of it, in which case it might be time to learn, and do, something new. Go for everything in life you want – at any age. A tiny home lifestyle can become an integral part of this post-retirement plan, allowing you more time and freedom to peruse the things in your life that really matter and that truly make you happy.

The Sandwich Generation

There is a large need in housing for those who are still caring for their children and suddenly have to also start caring for aging parents. This is generally called the sandwich generation.

Over 20% of US baby boomers (born between 1946 and 1964) could be in the position of having their parents and their children or grandchildren living with them, all at the same time. These multi-generational families are in need of more and varied living spaces. They are perfect candidates for tiny homes. One of the extended family members could live in a tiny house in the backyard, for example. Gives them space, keeps them close, and generally will contribute to a happier extended-family living situation.

Semi-assisted Living Individuals

There are times in our lives when we all need help. That may be in the form of assisted living and we might need it at any age. This could include after surgery or not being able to fully function during a recovery period.

Semi-assisted living might also be a situation where a parent or someone we know is simply not ready for a nursing home. They are able to take care of themselves and want their independence. However, it would be convenient and a lot of peace-of-mind to have them close by. A tiny home in your backyard might make all the difference.

Most assisted living facilities today cost an average of $3,000 to $5,000 per month. At this rate, it doesn't take many months before you could own a tiny house free and clear.

Extended Family

Tiny homes might be especially valuable for a parent, family or dear friend who want to live close by or have a place to stay when they visit for extended periods of time.

This doesn't mean this person is poor or lacking in finances because they might live in a tiny home. They might be quite well off but, as we know, money isn't everything. Close relationships can be worth more then money. To have a grandparent helping to raise your children might bring a wisdom, family history, and transgenerational bond that literally extend your family.

Tiny homes can often be put on existing lots as a granny unit, without having to purchase a separate lot. Check with your local zoning board. These are called Granny Flats in California. In Canada this is often called a codicil house, meaning co-domicile. It might just give someone you love a chance to stay close and a little extra something to wake up for each morning.

Single Professionals

There is an undeniable trend away from being married for the majority of our population. The new American way is single, and this isn't just due to divorce. It's also due to delayed marriages, cohabitation, and longer life spans. The demographic trends show the need for a new approach toward smaller houses. Tiny homes can provide a fitting option to a growing portion of our population.

Most single professionals don't need, or want, big houses and yards. So they tend to end up in condos or apartment buildings where there often isn't much individual expression or outdoor space. Tiny houses can offer an upscale environment with a small lawn and garden of your own without breaking the bank (and body) caring for a huge property.

Separated & Divorcees

Is it time to live on your own again? Need time and space to decide what to do about what isn't working anymore in your relationship or life? Tiny homes might be one viable solution. Cheaper than a second home and with more time and freedom to focus on the other aspects of your life that you need to pay the most attention to.

Newlyweds

Let's face it: when you're in love, you can't be too close to your sweetie — at least in the beginning. Thomas Jefferson did just that. Beginning in 1770, he lived in a two-story 18-foot by 18-foot, 648 square foot tiny home with only 324 square feet per level. This let him live on site while he built, and rebuilt, his great Virginian home, Monticello.

Jefferson used the upstairs as a bedroom and office and the basement as a kitchen and living room. Thomas lived in his tiny home alone for about two years. Then he brought his bride, Martha Wayles Skelton Jefferson, to join him. For three more years they lived together there, and called their tiny home the "honeymoon cottage."

Newlyweds can take Jefferson's lead and start their married lives together in a tiny home. You won't need to go into major debt with a huge mortgage, and you'll have more time and energy to spend with the new love of your life – it's a win-win!

Single Parents With (or Without) Kids

As a parent, there may be times you simply need another bedroom or space of your own without the noise, clutter and confusion of enthusiastic children. If you want your kids (and their friends) close, but not in your face, check out tiny homes.

There are some parents who have their children with them only infrequently, maybe due to custody arrangements. A tiny home can be a very viable option for parents who have their children part-time. With dual-purpose space and furniture, and many lofts and nooks, tiny homes can easily expand to fit a couple of extra bodies for any period of time.

Starter Homes

A tiny home is great as a starter home that can be designed for future additions and framed such that add-ons are easy and cost effective. For example, a window opening can be framed to become a future doorway leading to a new room. Additions can be added with only minor modifications when more space is needed, and more money becomes available.

Student Housing

Put a tiny house, or a cluster of them, on an existing lot in your kid's college town. Then rent it to your genius offspring and enjoy a tax write-off while you rent it to them. Upon graduation you can either sell the house or move it to a new location. This gives a cost-efficient place for the scholar to live, and they usually have great re-sale value, a possible tax deduction and real estate value appreciation for you.

Newly Graduated

Okay, your kid earned a degree, but can't find a job. What else to do but come back home till something pans out. A tiny house gives them a place to land, while preserving your peace; a not-so-empty nest.

Bed and Breakfast Expansion

Need an extra bedroom to rent out? Tiny homes offer a cost effective and profitable way to add rooms without adding an expensive expansion of the main house. In many historic homes and districts, it may not be possible to add on, but putting a tiny home out back may be perfectly acceptable. Be sure to check local zoning codes first.

Rental Income

Tiny homes can be rented, usually for the same amount, or more, as premium efficiencies. They can be an easy way to generate passive income on land you already own. Wouldn't an extra $500, or more, per month come in handy?

Home Office & Professional Space

Home office and professional spaces (massage, consultation, computer station) are perfect candidates for a tiny house. Do you need a separate place where you can work, concentrate and keep your office intact without kids or other interference? Walk to your office instead of driving for miles. Keep in mind, the current U.S. tax code allows 100% deduction for detached home offices.

Recreational and Vacation Getaways

Oh, those romantic cottages in the woods or next to a lake we all dream about. "Honey, let's get away for a few days – just the two of us." You can often build or set tiny houses on sites where "regular" houses might not be possible to build, such as on some lakefront property, out in the woods, or near a beach.

Tiny homes make a lot of sense as a vacation home or special getaway for a family. They're cheaper, more efficient, and the perfect amount of space when you need a break from your regular place.

Benefits of Tiny Houses

Who doesn't want to have more time, freedom, and money in their lives? We all do! Freedom can come from the time you don't have to spend in maintaining your house. It can also come in the form of being able to work less because you have smaller bills to pay. Tiny homes offer a path to freedom in many different forms.

Just the sheer size of today's McMansions means that families often require two incomes, sometimes even more, in order to pay the mortgage. Families often complain about the lack of money to meet their standard of living, yet they fail to do the one thing that will almost guarantee they can live within their means — and that is to sell their big house and downsize to one that is more suited to their needs and income.

Of course, there are circumstances in which a large home makes good sense. For example, if you have a huge family. Other times large houses fit is when money isn't an issue, or you need extra rooms for your office, at-home business, artist studio, workspace, or workshop.

An extended family occupying a three generation home used to be normal. This might be coming back into style. These were common well into the 20th century, when three and sometimes even four generations shared a house. New housing designs can accommodate multi-generations with in-law apartments, granny flats, nursery, and teenager suites.

Yet, if you do not need to house many people, a smaller home can help you reevaluate how to spend your time and money and directly affect the amount of freedom in your life.

You can take pride in learning how much is enough and in accepting the freedom of voluntary simplicity. In the end, you will have quality things that serve you, rather than a large number of things that own you.

There is an element of self-esteem, self-sufficiency, pride, and independence that can come with living in smaller homes. It's an inner power rather than a display of external trappings. It's self-knowing. It's being rich by having enough, wealth by contentment.

In America today, placing such emphasis on the size of one's home has taken on an ugly connotation that if we live in a large house, we are successful. Conversely, if we live in a small home, we are often thought of as being inferior or poorer than those who live in a big house. This implies we don't earn enough money. From that view, anyone could get an inferiority complex from such thinking about simple, small-space living.

Authentic power is not wrapped up in external items that we often get for show and to impress others. A big paycheck doesn't have to translate into a big house and lots of things. You can't buy self-esteem, a good reputation, or even true friends.

Below are some real reasons why living smaller can help promote an improved lifestyle.

Smaller Mortgage Payments than for a big house.

Lower Property Taxes.

Less Space to Heat and Cool — year after year — this saves you big bucks on heating and air conditioning bills.

Less Use of Electricity. Tiny homes tend to have fewer rooms with more natural lighting. They tend not to require as much artificial light as larger homes do.

Save on Building Costs. Building a new tiny house can save you tens of thousands of dollars because it takes less building materials than larger homes. This also helps conserve the Earth's ecology, forests and non-renewable resources.

Less Construction Time. There is less construction time required to build a smaller home. It takes much less time to build a 1,000 square foot house than it does a 3,000 square foot house. This saves on construction loan interest and decreases rental time or payment on your previous residence.

Financial Independence. You can achieve financial independence faster by paying down a smaller mortgage, lowering property taxes, and having smaller continuing monthly utility and maintenance expenses. We define financial independence when passive income (from investments, rentals, royalties) is equal to, or greater than, your expenses.

Travel. Leaving a smaller house for weeks or months has much less preparation, cleaning or consideration compared to larger houses. Set the thermostat on minimum and save money on heating or air conditioning the smaller space while you travel.

Fewer Worries. If something really goes wrong with your house, when a disaster strikes (hurricane, tornado, flood, fire) then you don't have as much to lose as you would with a big house. Repairs (roof replacement, window replacement, siding repairs) cost less and can be done much more quickly.

Smaller is Easier to Clean. This is a real no-brainer. Fewer windows to wash and less square footage to vacuum. More time to do the things you actually enjoy doing.

The process of building a house can be very daunting. With a tiny home it's less of a big operation. Here's why.

Land Preparation. One of the first ways you can save money is on land preparation. It is entirely possible to build one of these little houses on piers that are dug by hand or with a posthole digger attachment on a farm tractor.

Cost of Building Materials. A second big way you can save money with a tiny house is in the overall cost of the building materials. It simply does not take that many boards, nails, windows and doors to build an honest little house.

Smaller Appliances. Third, appliances don't have to be full-size or extraordinarily expensive. Even if you add an energy-efficient washer and dryer, you can buy all the appliances you need for less than $2,000.

Heating and Cooling Options. In many instances, you won't need central heating and air conditioning. You can get by very nicely with a small, vented, propane fireplace for heat, and a window air conditioner for cooling, especially if you have designed and situated your little house to take advantage of passive solar heating and cooling.

In a more elaborate scenario you can use one of the through-the-wall heat pumps, which both heats and cools, depending on your needs. For someone who really wants to have a feel of hominess, a small wood-burning stove with a glass front, which allows you to see the flames, is a nice touch.

Upgraded Bathroom. Since you will probably have only one or two bathrooms, you can splurge a bit on the fixtures. Instead of just an ordinary tub, you can look at putting in one of the whirlpool tubs, and justify the cost to well-body maintenance. A soothing whirlpool bath can do wonders for massaging sore and aching muscles and for relieving stress.

You might also consider adding an outdoor shower for use in the warmer weather. There is something positively energizing about a hot shower in the open air with the sun or moon shining down. Certainly if you are in a populated area you will want to build an enclosure around your outdoor shower, but it doesn't have to be elaborate, just minimally shielding from neighboring eyes.

A stylish enclosure can be made with decay-resistant wood such as red cedar. Add stainless steel piping and showerhead and it will be very attractive. It will be especially useful if you can access the outdoor shower from your bathroom, then you can leave your robe inside and step outside for the shower experience.

Not-So-Tall-House. Because your tiny house will be only one, or two, stories high, you may not be afraid to climb up "there" and do the maintenance chores that you might otherwise have to hire someone else to do on a full size house.

Painting & Exterior Maintenance. Painting is much easier and faster on a tiny house, and practically painless if you only do one side each year. Cleaning gutters, trimming shrubs, tending flowers in the window boxes, all require much less of your time when the house is smaller and has fewer shrubs and window boxes.

Tiny Houses on Wheels

Throughout the world and since the beginning of time people have moved with the seasons and have taken their tiny homes with them. Examples are yurts, tents, lodges, domes, tipis, and Conestoga wagons. For over a thousand years, gypsy wagons and caravans have traveled across Europe and the United Kingdom.

There is a need, and market niche for, tiny houses on wheels. Even though tiny homes on wheels are moveable, they are different from recreational vehicles (RV) in that tiny homes are not intended to travel down the highways at high speeds for extended periods. Rather, they are built to fully function as a home, with the added benefit of being able to relocate the entire structure, if necessary.

If you build your tiny home on a trailer, you can move it from property to property occasionally, and even across the country once or twice, if necessary. Once you locate it on the site where you choose to use the tiny home, you can either leave it on its trailer for easy moving in the future, or remove it from the trailer and set it on some form of foundation.

Designing and building a tiny house on a trailer differs in several ways from building one on a foundation. First, of course, you will have to consider transport restrictions and load limitations. For most federal and state highways, you can figure your combination of trailer and tiny house can be no more than 13 feet 6 inches tall. If you are moving your home just a short distance and are sure the area is clear of overhead wires and tree branches, you can exceed this limit somewhat.

You also have to keep the overall width of your portable tiny house within the restrictions established by your state. For example, in Virginia, any load over 10 feet wide and up to the 16-foot maximum width has to have an over-wide load permit and be accompanied by an escort vehicle in the front and another in the rear. The measurement is taken at the widest part of the house, generally the eaves.

Length is not so critical for over the road transport, unless your destination is at the end of a twisted little path where a long vehicle will have trouble negotiating the curves. Many of the park model tiny homes are 34 feet long with an attached 10 foot porch, making their overall length 44 feet. There are several modular home companies that can manufacture housing sections up to 66 feet long and transport them on specially built heavy-duty carriers.

Another consideration, if you are building your house on a trailer, is to make sure your plumbing, electrical and HVAC installation can accommodate the trailer framing.

You will also want to install some manner of water proofing membrane on the underneath so the floor insulation doesn't get wet if you move the trailer on a rainy day. Use heavy-duty plastic and staple it securely to the underneath of the floor joists as you install the floor on the trailer. Also, you will want to have shutters over the windows or some other form of protection to keep the windowpanes intact during transport. Unlike a car windshield, which is tempered glass, typical house windows are fragile and very likely to crack if hit by road gravel.

Don't use sheetrock inside a tiny house that is to be moved, because of the cracks in the sheetrock joints. Instead, use either solid pine logs or 1-inch × 6-inch tongue and groove eastern white pine boards which are very attractive.

The overall weight of the house is also a consideration when designing and building one for portability. If you are using a lightweight utility trailer, you are limited to about 7,000 pounds of house weight, which is easy enough to achieve if you use light framing materials and finish materials and if your house size isn't much larger than say 10-feet × 20-feet. Stay away from extra thick walls, heavy dimensional roof shingles and drywall, all of which are heavy and can be replaced by much lighter materials such as 2×2 walls, metal roofing panels, and pine interior walls.

If you are planning to build the house and then move it only one time, you can hire someone with a heavy-duty trailer and truck to move the house. You can lift the house onto the trailer, and then lift it onto your new foundation with a hired crane.

If you have built your tiny house on a trailer but don't want to hire a crane, haul the tiny house to your destination, then use jacks to lift the house clear of the trailer. Remove the trailer, then install the permanent piers and lower the house onto them.

You can learn a tremendous amount about space utilization and comfort by studying both the recreational vehicle industry and the recreational boating industry. Boat builders, RV manufacturers, and marine design engineers have gone all out to find ways to conserve space, provide storage and utility, and equip their cabins with the latest in technology to convert what might otherwise be a cramped, restrictive, dysfunctional shoebox into a spacious, comfortable, efficient, and fun living environment.

Not only is mimicking the artistry of ancient gypsy wagons and modern recreational vehicles useful in our tiny house design process, we can also use miniaturized RV support systems such as water and sewer mechanics, heating and air conditioning equipment, electrical systems, and transport systems as models of how we can use less energy for better results. These are all things that can inform our design process and make our tiny houses more livable and infinitely more enjoyable.

We can also learn from the construction sequences used by the RV manufacturers. They build the recreational vehicles indoors at a series of workstations that make up an assembly line. The unit moves from station to station where trained operatives perform tasks in sequence.

Much of the interior of the RV is actually finished before the outside skin is applied, thus saving in time and labor. Tasks can be performed from outside the building in a standing position.

When we look at recreational vehicles and compare them to tiny houses, it becomes very clear that the one true way to make housing less expensive is to make it smaller.

For example, in a typical new home of today, the master bedroom might be as large as 400 square feet, compared to a comfortable but compact master bedroom in a travel trailer that is only 64 square feet, including two shirt closets and a large storage compartment under the bed.

Nationally, there are nearly one million full-time and part-time RV residents who are doing wonderfully well in homes that are very much representative of the tiny house concept. Even the largest of the recreational vehicles have less than 300 square feet of living space. Many full-time RV folks are doing just fine in a traveling home containing less square footage than their former suburban living room. Probably two thirds of the full-timers travel from place to place, either following the sun or visiting as much of our beautiful country as possible. Other full-time RV residents park their travel trailer or motor home in a campground or on private land and live there full time, usually with semi-permanent connections to water, sewer and electricity.

These mobile tiny homes are legally classified under a category of recreational vehicle called park trailer. Park trailers have a wide range of possibility for semi-permanent and permanent housing. Legally, to be built on a trailer, they are no wider than 12 feet and no longer than 33 feet. The overall size of the park trailer cannot exceed 400 square feet. Park trailers are built on a trailer and towed to a permanent or semi-permanent site.

Because park trailers are built as recreational vehicles, it might be possible for you to park one on your land without a building permit. This is not a guarantee because zoning laws vary tremendously in different localities. Check with your local zoning officials. But if you can park it under the RV code, this means you probably don't need a permit to park it and don't necessarily have to buy another building lot which might be required with a permanent building.

Even though park trailers come under the recreational vehicle building guidelines, they are not meant to be towed day after day from site to site as is a travel trailer. They are just too bulky and not at all streamlined.

Financing is also available for the park models and they can qualify under the home equity loans as long as you own the land it will be sitting on. Check with your mortgage broker for plans and rates.

Park model tiny homes are either log cabin style, stick built, or built with structural insulated panels (SIPS). The SIPS and stick built units give the flexibility for the house to be finished to match the neighborhood where it will be parked or set. For example, if your main house has painted clapboard siding then you can use the same style and color clapboard siding on the tiny house to match and blend in with the larger house.

Smart, Stylish Bedrooms Ideas for Tiny Homes

The recent economic downturn has made many people cautious about investing in big homes. If you have a tiny home that you want to furnish in a stylish way, there is a lot to choose from. You need not compromise on space and style. You can easily create an illusion of space and make your home look big, beautiful, and well organized. There are clever ways to avoid clutter and add to the beauty of your bedroom by using some great designs available in the market, such as Murphy beds or lofted sleeping spaces. In no time at all, the limited space is an advantage, as it lets you have creative options like these to style your interiors. A hidden bed that can be folded back into a cupboard against the wall is an attractive way to make the most of the limited space you have.

When you pay attention to these design details, you will find that your home design goals become easier. You get a multifunctional room that has added storage area when you opt for a hidden bed. Now there's a win-win situation! In a single step, you get a comfortable sleeping space along with an elegant utilization of the space you do have. Efficiently using your space is a great way to avoid a lot of clutter. It will bring in a lot of fresh air and light into your room. You get to choose from a lot of different styles, designs and colors in these beds too.

An interesting look can be achieved in minimal space with a loft bed. These are excellent choices that offer not just a space to sleep in but also provide space for storage underneath. The loft bed doesn't fold into the wall. Instead, it pulls down from the ceiling giving a feeling of being on a floating bed, or is built permanently closer to the ceiling, with stairs or a ladder to access the space. It even gives you space underneath it even while you use it for storing without any inconvenience. Isn't that a great idea to use in your bedroom? I love the idea of being able to reach for a book or a drink while relaxing up on my bed, no wasting of space, and quite trendy, too.

A bedup is yet another option which can be considered for your home. The structure works very simply by being pulled up to create a sort of false ceiling when not in use. You can add definition to the room with this design style and can use some interesting lighting on the false ceiling to add to a great look. It adds to the decorative look and can contribute with spatial accents that will complement the overall look you are creating in your bedroom.

Bring in a lot of mirrors to add to the beauty of your bedroom, play with textures and colors to create a plush look. You can have a functional and comfortable living space that makes you feel like your home is your palace. Keep in mind that light hues create a better illusion of space than dark ones do when choosing your final look.

Kitchen Options in Tiny Houses: Working Well in a Tiny Kitchen

Cooking in a small, cozy space of your own can be quite a fun and relaxing task. It is easy to reach everything you need if you plan and construct the right kind of shelves and cabinets for your kitchen. There are fewer distractions in a small kitchen, it doesn't provide for a lot of things to be spread out, this means less chances of cooking going wrong or a disaster happening. It is also neat and tidy and much easier to maintain. Cooking in a tiny kitchen allows you to clean as you work on each dish, without a lot of time being wasted. It is also much easier to work in, easier to find ingredients, and less tiring to reach for everything you need.

The most important decisions to be made are what equipment to pick for your kitchen and how to utilize the space available in the best way. Excessive equipment gathering dust and taking up the precious space is simply a waste. Instead just think of the bare essentials you will need to work with. Consider making some good sturdy cabinets to put away all the pots and pans, and avoid putting single use items into them. Question every item before you decide to buy it, so you get only what you really need to cook with.

Even many master chefs swear that a tiny kitchen is a great idea. Many folks find it enjoyable to cook and get that cathartic personal time to work in peace when they have a tiny kitchen. There won't be a lot of heads crowding in, no constant sampling, or distractions to take away your attention from the work, making it easy to quickly whip up some delectable dishes. Start by cutting down on the clutter of appliances that take up unnecessary space. Opt for only essential appliances like a smaller fridge, microwave, small oven, and food processor. Do away with extras like fancy coffee machines (a French press works perfect), ice cream machines, juicers, etc.; store them in cabinets or put them away unless they are a daily use appliance that you cannot do without.

There are many ways to create a roomier look for your kitchen. People are moving toward the idea of an open kitchen and doing away with the closed cabinetry and doors for kitchen spaces. Consider having open cupboards that have glass doors, which creates a roomier look for your storing space. You can choose between mesh screen doors or glass doors for the cabinets, both of which offer visibility and allow you to have enough room to put away things in. A great way to create an illusion of space is to have an open kitchen, when the kitchen opens out into an adjoining room either through a large window or by avoiding a wall, to make it look bigger. The important thing to consider is how to make every space available to you usable in a way where clutter is avoided.

Adding an accent to a tiny kitchen is easy and a great way to make it look stylish. Have hanging racks to put away the cutlery, glasses and smaller pots and pans. There are wall mountable magnetic spice and knife racks you can use to make the most of the limited space, creating a trendy look. If you have the time and interest, you can take up DIY projects like making magnetic racks with an old pizza pan or using wooden pegs to organize the cutlery.

There are plenty of easy to follow pictures and design instructions available online.

Hanging the pots and pans on the wall to create a tableau is also a great idea; it makes for easy reach and allows you more storage space in the cabinets. Consider having a slide out cutting board hidden away between the kitchen drawers. It can also be converted to a two-legged table with two backless stools you can pull out to have some coffee with company while cooking. Using backless stools or chairs without armrests is good in smaller spaces, as they are easy to tuck away and move around. Doing away with an island area in the kitchen is best, when there is limited space. Instead, ideas like these allow you to have that extra seating space without compromising on the space that is available.

You can add a pop of color by having the ceiling in a shade of turquoise, which also makes the space look bright and can create an illusion of being larger when done right. You can store cutting boards under the cabinets with a magnetic attachment too, if you like. This makes it also quite easy to reach as you are working in the small space. Cleaning materials can also be placed on the side of the cabinets, with a hook or magnetic attachment, making it easy to clear up after you work.

Lighting is of utmost importance in a kitchen, especially in a tiny home. Lighting, when done right, can create a wonderful look and make the space look bigger too. Avoid bulky lights or huge fixtures. Instead, use simple, subtle lighting under cabinets or the counter. Lights in the false ceiling in a kitchen also add to the look, creating better space. The kitchen will be adequately lit with these clever ideas and will also look roomier. Diagonal tiles for flooring can be added to the kitchen to create an illusion of length for the kitchen.

Another idea that works well when you want to make your kitchen look more spacious is to paint the cabinets of the kitchen the same as the color of the walls. The use of pale colors reflects light well, which is good for creating a spacious look but choosing darker shades like chocolate, navy or charcoal is not a bad idea. They visually create a feeling of the walls being farther back than they actually are. Working with the right colors and choosing good lighting for the space will help you with creating a good look.

Planning what you want to do with the available space and choosing to do away with what you don't require in your limited space will do wonders for your kitchen. When done right, it will be not just a place you love to cook in but it will feel like a lot of room for you to do all your work easily in.

Bathroom Options in Tiny Homes

A tiny bathroom space can be turned into a fine bathing area with a bit of planning and by carefully choosing interesting design elements. You have limited space to work with, so it becomes important to ensure you don't end up cluttering it up and having no room to turn and move about in. Aesthetics and beauty do not have to be compromised in smaller living spaces. In fact, there are often creative uses of simple elements to create a look that is trendy and useful. To start with, look at how each element in the bathroom interacts with the existing space. This will give you a good idea of whether each individual element is necessary or if it must be changed to a smaller one to create more space. The right sinks, showers, and lighting will make a lot of difference to your tiny bathroom. You can easily make it look and feel roomier with the right kind of fixtures. For instance, instead of having a shower curtain or shower doors, consider opting for an open bathroom with floor drains. This really makes the space well lit and roomy. Consider opting for a stand-alone sink, rather than a vanity mirror, or his and her sinks for the bathroom. Opt for a narrow pedestal sinks; this makes for easy, practical use while not taking away from the space.

Using rich, dark colors in the walls of the bathroom is a good idea if you have a lot of natural light coming in. It creates an illusion of space by causing the walls to recede when viewing it. Use ambient and task lighting; it adds to the cozy look and feel of the bathroom. You can also consider lighting in the form of wall sconces to add a bit of old school look. These lights come in creative designs with a nickel or brass finish, along with adjustable intensity and flexible neck. Add on a corner tub or a diagonal one rather than a long one to minimize the use of space. Using details like lines in a continuous horizontal design, frameless mirrors, and avoiding a curb for the shower is also a good way to maximize the illusion of space. If you have a vanity sink in the guest bathroom, consider adding on deep drawers under this to add more storage space. These will help to provide storage without a lot of things cluttering up the limited space in the bathroom. Classic diagonal tiling along with bold prints in wallpaper in the bathroom makes for a very elegant look.

Whether you are remodeling your bathroom or looking at getting a touch of style added, using some tiles in a contrast print or design is a good way to add backsplash without costing you too much. For tiny spaces, this makes for a good way to create an adornment without taking away from the space. It doesn't cost a lot to use few tiles just behind the sink area or beneath the mirror. A wall mount sink that is a narrow one also allows you to save on space while providing utility and a very stylish look for petite bathrooms. Playing with prints and creating attractive textures is a good idea. A rug with a blue print combined with a metallic stool allows you to add a bit of panache to the bathroom, cozying it up for a great look. Have navy colored wallpaper to match the whole look.

Colors are a good way to liven up the bathroom, Try something in green or blue, for a more aquatic, natural theme. (You can, of course, mix up the colors according to the color scheme of your bathroom). For a lime green bathroom, adding a mix of coral and green towels adds to the look. It also brightens up the room when detailing is done in light colors, creating a look of being well-lit. You can place a pretty basket on the wall to store bath salts, shampoo, bubble bath and other particulars near the window. You could also place it on the windowsill itself, saving space and having everything within easy reach for your use.

For more aesthetic ideas, look at interesting shelf and hook combos in the market. Use good organic lamps to hang just above the mirror along with quirky hand towel holders in order to add a dash of personality. These are great for making a style statement for an attractive look in the bathroom. When you have a stark white bathroom, consider adding interesting details like a seashell encrusted mirror to add a touch of class. The play with texture also allows for distraction, taking focus away from the size and to the interesting details in the bathroom that make it feel more rich.

Opt for secure and smart wall brackets for storage and, when space is limited, use a pretty mat on the toilet tank and use it as a ledge to put the essentials for your bath. Floating shelves are also an excellent idea in minimal space.

Going minimal is also smart if you are looking at fitting a tub into a tight space. In order to create an illusion of space in a small bathroom, add a mirror to the side of the tub while keeping other details minimal, to avoid clutter. Glass jars can be used to store your bath salts, ear buds, cotton balls, etc., keeping it free of moisture and dust while also creating a roomy, airy and fresh look to the bathroom. Store them in the wall bracket shelves to add accents to the look. Add in some simple display with a bunch of fresh flowers in a corner vase.

When you want low maintenance furniture for your bathroom, use stainless steel shelves mounted over the toilet, or steel storage cubes against the wall with rust resistant finish, which make for easy-to-use units that don't require a lot of work to maintain. If you don't have a lot of natural light coming into the bathroom, avoid the dark shades of color. Instead, stick to neutral, light pastel or white shades with color added here and there to create an interesting look.

The Problem with Stuff

How could one be richer? Not financially, but emotionally. Is there anything better or healthier than to be happy, and even joyful, the majority of the time? Prosperity is a conscious state of mind; it is not just about money. How many extraordinarily rich people have you heard about that ended up living lives without joy? Rich, but no friends. Alone, negative, miserly and miserable.

Stuff makes your home unique and expresses your individual personality. No big hairy deal. Everyone needs *some* stuff. But do we have too much stuff these days? The tiny house movement seems to think so. People are finding that they can lead much happier, more fulfilling lives by getting rid of the great majority of their *stuff* and living a more natural life. Just keep the stuff you want and get rid of stuff if it no longer serves you. It's a simple philosophy, with profound effects.

Think about the increasing popularity of the self-storage buildings. Most folks would rather rent a storage bin for $50 per month ($600 per year) than to sit down and methodically weed out their possessions. Yet, you can routinely see notices of self-storage units auctioned off because of nonpayment for the storage. But still, the industry is booming as people find it more and more difficult to part with any of their acquired things.

Your goal is not to deprive yourself of anything or any of your collections. Your goal is to free yourself of things you don't want, and things that no longer serve or please you. Here's some homework for you: Take an inventory of your possessions. Put them into two categories – Needs and Wants. Be honest with yourself. Are you surprised by how many things fall in the Wants category, and how few are in the Needs?

Think about the consequences of clutter in your life. If you had to move tomorrow, would you take all of your items with you? Would you pay to have them transported? Would you pay to store them? When was the last time you used all of those things?

There is a rule of thumb saying that if you don't use something for an entire year, then you probably don't need it. It is a great thing to do once a year and really helps you see and appreciate how little material goods we actually need. Let's take a look at some of the consequences of having too much *stuff*.

Financial Consequences of Stuff

- Bigger house & higher mortgage = thousands of dollars over the lifetime of the loan.

- Resale value of stuff = not much. Yard sales and auction prices.

- Money spent on stuff is money that is not in savings or investments = big time opportunity losses.

Social Consequences of Stuff

- Messy house causes you to be embarrassed to have folks over = lonely and isolated.

- Too much trouble to entertain because cleaning takes so long. Because you don't invite folks over they don't invite you either = lonely and isolated.

- You, or your estate, must ultimately deal with the stuff when you are no longer around.

- Sooner or later, it's the landfill = the ultimate grave for all your stuff.

Health Consequences of Stuff

- Dirty and messy house leads to molds and dust resulting in allergies, asthma and challenged immune system.

- Things on floor or steps can lead to accidents = higher insurance premiums.

- Clutter in cabinets can lead to dangerous spills. Prescription drugs fall out of medicine cabinet. Toxic cleaners spill on floor.

Environmental Consequences of Stuff

- Natural resources used to manufacture stuff. These are not never-ending sources.

- Packaging, shipping and handling = fuel and energy consumption.

- Tipping fees at landfills = environmentally insensitive.

Cleaning Clutter & Stuff

- Must move stuff to dust or clean.

- More expensive to clean.

- Takes more cleaning time because of volume.
- Bigger houses have more space for stuff = you buy more stuff to fill all of the empty space.

Frustration of Stuff
- Can't find things when needed. Lots of time spent looking.
- Blame your spouse or housemate for losing things
- Unpleasant argument and building tension lead to fighting or even separation.

Moving Day for Stuff
- Harder because more stuff.
- More expensive to move, multiple trips & bigger van, more muscular men needed.
- Harder to pack.
- More boxes & packing materials

Many people in the tiny house movement condemn the steady stream of "stuff" that is filling up our landfills. One way to interrupt this stream of junk is to stop buying stuff we don't need.

Things to Consider About Your Stuff

There are three main reasons we keep stuff. Considering and thinking about these might help you decide to pare down your belongings so you can fit into a tiny house.

Frequency of Use. If you look at a possession and can't remember the last time you used it, then get rid of it. If you have to put a number on it, then it's probably not very useful. Anything you haven't used for 12 months is fair game for disposal. But wait, you might think, I'll need it sometime in the future. Maybe that's true, but again, if you haven't used it for a year, chances are you aren't going to use it next year either.

Ego. We are often attached to our stuff because of ego. We paid a lot of money for the item and we feel guilty or embarrassed about selling it or giving it away for what it's really worth. Idle exercise equipment usually falls in this category. Every basement we can ever remember being in had at least one formerly high priced item that now has only 'ego' value. Let go of the ego, get rid of the stuff, and de-clutter your life.

Sentimental Reasons. The third reason we keep things is because we are sentimentally attached to them and it would just break our heart to have to part with them. Furniture from our parents and grandparents is a good example of this category. Some of these items can be easily and beautifully incorporated into a tiny house. Others can be given away to family members or friends, thus keeping it close by and in good hands.

Start Selling

So you need to or want to get rid of your stuff? Great. Here's one fun way you can. You can make this exercise into a little business venture. Use the money you earn from selling your excess stuff to fund an investment, or start a small, at-home, part-time business.

The mechanics of unloading your unused items are very simple: find out what it's worth and let it go. Here are a few ways to let it go.

1. Yard Sales

Yard sales are fun and can be useful if you are located in an area where there's a big enough population pool to attract to your sale.

2. Antiques Dealers

If you don't favor the idea of yard sales, then consider calling a local antiques dealer to have them look at your items to see if any of them have value. There is always a possibility that you will have something worth selling. How do you find a dealer who will treat you fairly? Ask around to see if any of your friends or relatives have suggestions. Most antiques dealers have a reputation in the community and will treat you fairly. If in doubt, ask for more than one opinion, and also look for your items in one of the books on antiques to see what the value might be.

3. On-line Auctions

Selling items on Internet auctions, and especially eBay, is easier in many ways than holding a yard sale. It's simple to open an account on eBay, and there is a tutorial you can follow to help you learn the ropes. All you then need is a digital camera or a photo scanner to load pictures of your items on to the eBay sales page.

4. Special Gifts for Special People

As you are moving down the list of items you want to get out of your house, you may find some things that have too much sentimental value to sell. Or, they don't have enough monetary value to make selling them worthwhile. In that case, give them away to someone special that shares your sentiment or values.

5. Non-profit Donations

The advantage to donating to charity and non-profit organizations is that you can get a receipt and deduct that amount from your taxes — right off the bottom line. Clothing is particularly welcome for use in inner city areas and overseas to clothe people in need.

6. Recycle

As you are cleaning out boxes, files and corners, keep in mind that many of the items might be recyclable. This includes glass jars, newspapers and magazines, old files, metal cans or old cars and other items. It might be an extra effort for you to sort and recycle, but it's worth it to help preserve our forests and keep recyclable materials out of the landfills.

Sometimes if you have a large item, such as an old car or piece of farm equipment, you can call a scrap metal dealer. They will sometimes come and pick up the item for free and sometimes you can get a tax deduction. Some municipal cities and counties have a junk car plan to help pick up old vehicles and keep the county looking tidier.

7. Burning & Releasing

It's very therapeutic to watch some things burn. Items you may release to the fire include:

- Old love letters.

- Clothes too large because of losing weight.

- Outdated tax forms and financial documents (make digital copies).

- Journals processing a difficult life passage or situation

You get the idea. It's great fun and a statement of your intent to make peace with the past.

How to Organize Your Stuff

Now that you've pared down your possessions to what you feel is a reasonable level that serves you and your new lifestyle, it's on to the next step. Now you can decide how you are going to store or closet the stuff you are keeping or taking with you to your tiny home. Any of the home improvement stores carry several styles of inexpensive closet organizers that are great for bringing order to chaos. Study them carefully, keeping in mind how much closet space you have available and the items you wish to store there.

If you find that even after diligently de-junking your life, you still need more storage space than your little house has, then consider buying or building a small storage building in your backyard.

In most areas of the country you can buy a little storage shed and have it delivered to your home for less than $1,000. This is certainly a better investment than to rent a similar size storage bin at $50 or $100 per month, year after year. When you rent one of those self-storage units, you will be helping to pay the mortgage and make a profit for the guy who owns the self-storage yard, instead of improving the value of your own property.

Going Green

We've already discovered the many ways that a tiny house makes economic sense, now let's explore how tiny houses can make good ecological sense as well. Is it possible that we can use tiny houses to help heal some of the environmental challenges we face? The answer is a resounding yes!

There are many major areas of concern that weave together and form the web of all creation. Here you can be primarily concerned with the ones that are a result of the unintended consequences of our nation's conventional 'bigger-is-better' housing orientation.

- Reduced air quality
- Reduced water quality
- Forest degradation
- Wildlife habitat destruction
- Excessive fossil fuel energy consumption
- Soil erosion
- Declining food quality
- Excessive materials waste
- Declining plant diversity
- Declining animal diversity
- Compromised human health and well-being

It is beyond the scope of this book to delve deeply into how each area impacts the other or how they randomly, as well as synergistically, create the environment of our lives. However, the two questions it is important to address are: Could it be that our housing choices are ruining our quality of life? And, is it really necessary to use so many of our precious natural resources in the housing industry?

Large houses of today have a direct impact on our planet's ecology. There is no denying that, no matter how much you love your McMansion. For starters, the building of millions of large homes has an affect on the use of natural resources. Here's how:

Raw Materials, Manufacture and Transport. More oil is required and pollution generated to gather raw materials and manufacture building materials. More reliance on long distance transport for materials and supplies. Long distance transport requires heavy trucks, freight trains and ships. The long distance transport of the materials used to build these houses creates massive air quality concerns. The smokestack and exhaust pipe effect covers most of our planet now, with increased smog, lower air quality, higher incidence of respiratory ailments, and increased costs of air pollution mitigation. Here are just a few examples.

Most of the ceramic tile used in America's new homes comes from Europe, brought here by ship, or from Mexico, brought to the US by tractor trailer trucks that often don't meet clean air and safety standards set for US trucks. Hardwood lumber used in furniture, flooring, cabinets and wall paneling often comes from Asia, Latin America or South America, usually from tropical and sub-tropical forests that will never recover from the devastation of reckless clear-cutting. Much of the spruce dimensional lumber and nearly half of the plywood and oriented strand board that is used in the United

States comes from clear-cut forests in Canada. Many thousands of miles removed from where the lumber is cut to where it is used.

Clear Cutting Forests. Whenever clear cutting is allowed, the resulting soil erosion into the creeks and rivers causes serious consequences in silting and streambed alterations that will impact the native species and lower the water quality.

Larger Blight Created on Landscape. If we continue to build 2 million new homes in the U.S. per year, each averaging 2,200 square feet, we will exhaust our prime forestry resources within the next 20 to 40 years. Indeed, we have already exceeded our national forest growth rate. The bulk of our dimensional framing lumber is imported from Canada, where clear-cutting forests is not only allowed, but is encouraged by the government. The average house uses an amount of lumber roughly equivalent to a 5 acre clear-cut. Just in the United States, we are building an average of 2 million new homes per year, necessitating the clear-cutting of some 6 million acres of land each year. That is an astonishing amount.

The forest and lumbering industry will argue that they are replanting forests after clear-cuts, and that natural regeneration occurs beginning immediately. This is true to some extent. But, for the most part, the trees they are planting (soft woods) are of a single species and are more suited to the production of pulp for newsprint than for the production of good building materials. Hardwood is usually purchased from developing countries that rely heavily on the income from timber harvesting to meet their international debt and to pay the political costs of maintaining their government. In many third world countries, only a tiny portion of the earnings from timber harvesting actually go to help support the people. Often these valuable tropical hardwoods are harvested in a destructive way, leaving behind ecosystems that will never fully recover from the devastation. In this all-out pursuit of short-term gains, the long-range ramifications are incalculable.

Water Quality. Clear-cutting, combined with dams, whether for flood control or for hydroelectric power production, results in steadily declining fish populations, and a deteriorating quality of life for all animal species, including humans. Rivers and streams run brown with topsoil as a consequence of clear cutting forestland. It is predicted that topsoil will be one of the most valuable commodities in the future. Without topsoil, farmers cannot grow healthy crops. It will be a sad state of affairs when farmers have to worry about buying soil in order to grow the crops we depend on, but, sadly, we're not too far away from that day.

Decrease in Food Producing Land. In America, hundreds of thousands of acres of valuable farmland are being used each year to grow the ultimate crop: houses. How much of our farmland can we destroy and still continue to be able to feed ourselves?

Greater land disturbance as a result of the larger footprint of houses, attachments, and garages. More land area is required for larger septic systems to accommodate a greater number of bedrooms per house.

Affordable Homes. Higher house costs limit the number of people who can afford to buy.

Higher Heating and Cooling Costs. More energy is required to heat and cool large houses. The over-large homes that are so ubiquitous today demand a great deal of energy to assemble the materials and erect the house. But the ongoing costs for heating and cooling can reach tragic proportions. We are hearing more and more reports that heating and cooling bills are taking as much as 20% of the family's after tax income. This energy, for the most part, comes from oil and coal fired electricity-generating stations. The extraction and burning of coal and oil both have serious environmental consequences.

Higher Maintenance Costs. Larger homes have higher maintenance costs, including more labor and materials required for maintenance.

Higher Percentage of Income Spent on Housing. More time is spent earning the money to pay for the house. In all but the richest of households, a major portion of the family income is spent on housing. The higher the percentage of income spent on housing, the lower the household's remaining ability to spend for food, health care, recreation, retirement savings and investments.

There are ways to build homes with less impact on our environment. Reducing the size of the home is the first step, followed by choosing environmentally sensitive green building materials that have the least overall impact. Although many green materials are not yet standard or easy to obtain within the US, there are many available that are very effective for home construction and also effective for conserving our valuable resources of forests, animal diversity, air and water quality, and human health and wellbeing.

Can we, as a culture, embrace and utilize small and tiny homes to help give folks a quality life-style, while at the same time conserve energy and water, save our forests, preserve top soils and conserve farm lands? The answer is yes!

Alternatives to Building with Wood

In many parts of the country, wood is a readily renewable resource. In the Southeast and the South, for example, southern yellow pine is favored for dimensional lumber, especially useful for pressure treating for use in outdoor structures such as decks and porches. In the Northeast, eastern white pine and eastern white cedar are readily available for dimensional framing, interior finish, and siding. For the most part, these trees will reseed themselves so that the forest continues to produce useful building material.

The problem, however, is that in many areas, the timber companies are re-planting huge areas with tree species that are useful for paper pulp production but not for dimensional building lumber. In a generation or so there will be shortages of lumber to build new homes, even in states that have traditionally been net lumber producers and exporters.

It is important, then, that we turn our attention to either growing proper forests, or finding materials that we can successfully substitute for lumber. There are a number of building methods that lessen the need for lumber including; straw bale, cob, clay, papercrete, bamboo cob, adobe, rammed earth and so on.

Unfortunately, other than in a few isolated municipalities, most of these alternatives have not yet been approved, either by building codes or by banks. If you can't get a building permit then you can't get a bank loan, which means you will have to finance the building of your new home on your own. Many people have chosen to do just that, and it becomes a problem if they ever decide to sell their alternative house and move away. Then, any buyer who is interested in living in an alternative structure is faced with the same challenge, how to finance the purchase.

Builders can make it a part of their mission to use materials that are considered green and that are, at the same time, approved for use under the International Residential Building Code. In doing so, home builders can do as much as possible to ensure that homes have the least possible impact on the Earth, while still making it possible for the new homeowners to obtain all the necessary permits and bank financing. In addition, the materials we use are chosen for their performance and for their recycled content.

There are hundreds, even thousands, of green alternative building materials on the market that aren't terribly more expensive than the traditional and conventional materials that they replace.

Rather than try to cover the enormous range of green building products available, let's focus on just a few to give you an idea of the potential within the green movement.

Hardwood products one usually finds in a new home are furniture (both frames and finish material), flooring, and cabinets. A high percentage of the hardwood utilized, especially the clear, knot free grades, requires trees that are a hundred or more years old.

Bamboo

Like trees, bamboo is considered an agroforestry product, even though it is a member of the grass family. Like the fescue in your yard, it is an extremely high yield renewable resource. Bamboo has countless uses; food, animal fodder, garden stakes, fishing rods, construction materials such as wall paneling and flooring, paper pulp, fuel briquettes, furniture and musical instruments just to name a few.

Long lengths of bamboo can be inserted to reinforce poured concrete, and hollowed bamboo stems can be used for gutters to move water from your roof to your storage system.

Bamboo products are available in natural beige or amber colors. The natural light tones give a warm ambiance to the room, which is one reason we prefer the natural blonde color that highlights the node intersections of the bamboo. The pale cream-yellow color blends well with earth-toned wall paints and colorful fabrics, making interior decorating easy and delightful.

In some areas bamboo flooring is less expensive than hardwoods and it is readily available at a growing number of distributors. Most bamboo construction products are made from strips. Bamboo is hollow in the middle with walls that can be more than an inch thick. The strips are boiled in a natural non-toxic insect repellent.

The strips are then kiln dried and laminated to create a solid piece of flooring that is pre-finished and measures 5/8" thick, 3" wide and 36" long.

Bamboo is a member of the grass family. There are over 3,600 species of bamboo grown worldwide. Bamboo grows worldwide from the tropics, sea level and on snow-capped peaks. It is native to almost all continents.

Bamboo is one of our planet's fastest growing plants. Some of these immense tropical bamboos grow as much as two feet in a day! Timber bamboos can reach heights of 164 feet and have a base of 12 inches, and do that in less than 10 years.

Unlike trees, bamboo does not have to be replanted after harvest. Like other grasses, mature bamboo groves have extensive root systems that continue to send up shoots for decades.

There are two major classifications of bamboo. One is the runner (monopodia) bamboo that rapidly spreads. The other is the clumping (sympodial) bamboo that is non-invasive and grows in clumps.

Once a grove is established, bamboo can be harvested in as little as 4 years rather than the 30-60 years necessary to grow a softwood tree (pines) and the 60-120 years for a hardwood tree.

Harvesting is often done by hand which minimizes the impact on the local environment. Bamboo farmers understand the growth patterns and have the incentive to maximize timber production while maintaining healthy forests.

Bamboo is a good crop to grow on small acreage. Three to ten acres can yield much bamboo. Because of this, there are bamboo farmers establishing groves all across the U.S. and Canada.

Bamboo can also be utilized as animal fodder with a protein content of 18% to 28% depending on the species and time of year. In many cultures, bamboo is routinely harvested as fodder for livestock, especially in winter and during drought years.

Bamboo is so versatile and so viable a replacement for many hardwood and paper products that we wonder why trees should even be cut at all, much less clear-cut. How much healthier would our air be if trees were viewed as oxygen generators and left alone while we used a species of grass (bamboo) for much of our construction and paper needs.

Water

Water is one of the world's most valuable resources and it will become even more precious as more and more of it becomes polluted and unusable. Already, bottled water — at over $1/quart — is two times more expensive than gasoline. People who once took water for granted are rethinking their supply and its sources. In many parts of the country reservoirs, which were once consistently full, are now at record-level lows, if not dry.

In some portions of the country drought conditions are chronic. Wells in some regions of the country are no longer being replenished from natural underground storage aquifers. In all too many cases these aquifers are becoming polluted as more and more man-made chemicals seep further and further into the earth. The planet's population is growing to record numbers bringing dramatically increased water demands along with the increase in pollution.

Water is so critical to our health and quality-of-life. Every home needs water no matter what size or location. So what about that old-fashioned idea of rainwater harvesting? Years ago almost everyone did rainwater harvesting in some form or another. The old rain barrel was a common sight. This was virtually free water, costing nothing to harvest and very little to store once the initial cost of the cistern was paid.

An added benefit is that rainwater is distilled, perfectly "soft" water. There is no need for a water softener. It doesn't contain the minerals found in ground water nor does it contain the chemicals, including chlorine, often found in municipal treated water.

Rainwater is ideal for watering the garden, washing the car, doing laundry, and is perfect for potable uses once it is properly filtered.

A simple rainwater collection system can be as simple and cheap as a recycled metal or plastic drum placed under a downspout. Garden stores sell 55 to 75 gallon plastic and fiberglass rain barrels from $50 to $250. The more elaborate barrels come with leaf screens, spouts, and tubes to connect multiple barrels together in series.

To prevent mosquitoes from breeding in the water just make sure the barrels are covered or have a screened top. Also, a tablespoon of vegetable oil added into the water occasionally will help keep mosquitoes at bay.

A complete rainwater system including cisterns (storage tanks) and piping the water into your house is a little more complicated and expensive than a barrel under the downspout. The equipment you need includes special types of roofing, gutters, leaf screens, storage tank(s), filters, and a pump. Above or below grade systems are available. Above ground storage tanks have the advantage of easy maintenance, but are liable to freeze in cold weather. Underground tanks buried below the frost line will not freeze, but you will need a manhole access to be able to clean the tank and service the pump periodically.

Galvanized aluminum metal roofing is the best roof covering for collecting potable water because the surface is smooth and non-toxic. Asphalt, chemically treated wood shingles and some painted metal roofs can leach toxic materials. Be sure to have the water tested before drinking.

Even with a tiny house, you can collect rainwater; more than you might think. Anyone can benefit from learning how to capture and store water. It is usually cheaper than drilling a well and the water quality of rainwater is often better than that of many municipal systems and many ground water sources. Rainwater is naturally distilled by nature's evaporation and condensation process.

Even if you rely on an existing connection to the municipal system, or an existing well, you can still benefit by harvesting water and storing it for use in your garden and fishponds.

Rainfall lands on our rooftops anyway, and we have to have some form of guttering system to channel the rainfall away from our houses or we run the risk of water damage to our buildings. Adding a cistern or small reservoir to store the channeled rainfall is a simple and inexpensive way to harvest water that would otherwise run off our property with little benefit.

Seasonality of rainfall is a concern in some cases. In the Northwestern United States for example, rain falls mostly from late fall through spring, with very dry summers. If you are in one of those regions it may not be possible to harvest enough water in the winter to last you all summer.

The only way you will know is to determine how much water you actually need, and then see if you can harvest and store that much during the rainy season.

In the dry southwestern United States areas though, summer rains are infrequent, so it's not unusual for water harvesters in those regions to count their storage capacity in thousands of gallons instead of hundreds.

Calculating the amount of rainfall that would be available for you to harvest is simple. First, determine the roof area within your site that is available for water harvesting. Measure this roof area on the flat, not the slope.

Next multiply the result times the average number of inches of rain per month or per year and you will be able to see what your potential water harvesting capabilities are.

A typical household using all available water conserving techniques can easily get by with 50 gallons of water per day, so a 1,500 gallon storage tank is more than adequate for a one month supply. However, if you are in an area where two or three months can go by without an appreciable rain storm then you'll want to have two or even three 1,500 gallon tanks for storage.

You might think that all these tanks and related piping and filters will be too expensive to consider. Compared to the cost of drilling and developing a well, however, water-harvesting equipment can be a bargain. Even a simple well can cost over $7,500 for drilling, casing, piping, pump and pressure tank.

The water harvesting capability of your house is something you will want to consider during the design phase. From this standpoint you will want to have as much roof surface as possible. Whereas you may have been thinking about building a two story house to limit the size of the footprint, you may now want to consider building just a one story home with the same square footage but a larger footprint from which to harvest water.

You will also want to cover your roof with a material that lends itself to water harvesting. Impervious surfaces such as slate, certain kinds of plastic, and metal are preferred. We discourage the use of asphalt and Fiberglass singles because they are apt to shed particles into the water that you will then have to filter out.

Almost everyone at first recoils at the idea of rainwater harvesting because of fear the water might somehow be dirty. Bacteria and particles can be washed into your water from bird droppings landing on the roof, insects, airborne particulates and larger organic materials such as windblown seeds, leaves and twigs, acorns and nuts.

An important component in any rainwater harvesting is the roof washer. The first 50 gallons or so of rainwater flushes the particulates off the roof and that first 50 gallons is then diverted to a self-flushing holding tank before clean water is allowed to enter your storage tank. Before water is removed from the cistern for household use, it passes through a set of filters that are designed to filter out the larger particles first. Bacteria are then removed in a second filter.

Even the place you shelter your storage tank can provide a roof surface that adds to your water harvesting capacity. For example, the fresh water storage tank will be housed in a utility room on the back of the cottage. The utility room will have the water heater, water tank, filtering system, and battery and electrical equipment for the solar electric system. The room will measure 12-feet × 12-feet, with a 2-foot solar overhang on the roof edge. This roof adds 16-feet × 14-feet = 224 square feet to the water harvesting ability, and can capture nearly 150 gallons of water per one inch of rain.

One note of importance is that some lending institutions will be reluctant to place a mortgage loan on a house or property that relies on anything other than a municipal water system or approved well.

Storage Tanks

Place harvest tanks downstream of your collection system rather than trying to pump water upstream in a heavy storm. Place your primary storage tank downhill, and add a gravity-fed discharge pipe large enough to handle the overflow volume once your storage tank is full.

This discharge pipe can feed into a secondary surge tank below the first holding tank. That surge area can be a pond or rain garden or simple swale in your yard, or even your garden. Do whatever you can to keep the water on your site until it seeps into the ground. Don't let it simply drain into the roadside ditch and run off without first benefiting your site to the greatest possible extent. Have your garden beds arranged so that water can move freely along the pathways and seep into the beds adjacent to the pathways. Even if the water pools temporarily in your garden pathways it will soon percolate down to the root zone where it can be picked up and used by your plants.

Ponds

Another way to store rainwater harvested from your roof is in a fresh water pond in your yard. This is really no different than putting a pump and intake line into an existing lake, pond or creek, except that in a pond that you build yourself you more easily control the environment.

In summary, by overcoming a few challenges such as protecting lines from freezing in some areas, rainwater harvesting can be an easy, resourceful, and in many cases adequate method of acquiring water.

You may or may not be able to rely solely upon it for all household consumption. It depends on your total water consumption needs, average rainfall in your locale, and the ability of your home's roof surface to harvest water.

Tiny Home - The Alternative House Opportunity

People have focused on how tiny houses can be upscale, dignified, handcrafted and magical. They offer many advantages for simpler lifestyles. It has already been discussed how the size of your home does not necessarily reflect your wealth. For many of us, our housing situation is simply a matter of choice that is determined by what suits our personal tastes.

However, there are millions who are living in homes that do not serve them well. Many folks in the world are "inappropriately housed" as they have houses that are inappropriate for their lifestyle. This might be because a house is too big, too small, too old, too broken, too expensive, too inaccessible. There are many reasons how and why a house might be inappropriate for the inhabitants.

There are other individuals and families who simply have no home at all. This might be because they have fallen on hard times, or have been displaced due to natural or political instability.

Many inappropriately housed and unhoused people might benefit from an alternative selection in housing. Our cultural standard has become the 2,000+ square foot, three bedroom, two bathhouses with two car garages.

So we ask: can tiny homes provide a niche and "alternative" housing opportunity that none of the other available housing options currently offer?

It is the belief of the tiny house movement that the answer to this question is unequivocally "yes".

Tiny homes might provide an alternative housing choice for those who simply do not need, nor want, the standard three bedroom single-family house or the mini-mansion. Less of a house is often desired by young adults just beginning or by seniors who cannot, or do not wish to care for more space than they need.

For example, a tiny home may be more appropriate for the well-to-do middle class widower who currently lives in a super-sized house that was appropriate for bringing up a family, but now is, obsolete for her current life phase. Additionally, she may no longer have enough energy, time, or know-how to maintain the property properly.

What some people really might prefer is a smaller home close to support groups of friends or family. The problem is that few such houses exist in the current market place. For the wealthier segment of our population, the substitute for support groups is the "extended care retirement communities." This supplies institutional support and community by proxy. But this type of housing is very expensive and out of reach for many senior citizens.

It is not only senior citizens who might benefit from alternative housing. Tiny homes may provide appropriate, alternative housing to a wide variety of people in a variety of situations such as we presented earlier?

Here is something to ponder. If it is true that "home is where your heart is" and if your heart is homeless, then there is probably a part of you that is searching for appropriate housing. If available, that heart-felt home would probably be close to friends, family and support groups.

Tiny homes may help to house the unhoused by providing a "just-right" housing alternative to those who lack access to an affordable, simple, decent dwelling. Below we have outlined a few ways tiny houses might provide "alternative, affordable housing", and also possible scenarios that provide housing solutions for some of our society's problems.

Tiny houses placed on existing lots might provide a housing opportunity and safety-net that is not available anywhere else in society. A tiny home helped reunite a family and had ramifications from teaching his nephews guitar to helping around the house and with the family business.

Tiny homes might provide alternative housing to folks who are perhaps just down on their luck, between jobs, in need of downsizing, or who need rehabilitation while they recover from an accident or disease. Sometimes these individuals might find just the self-esteem boost needed when they have a decent place to live while they face their life's traumas and challenges.

Many individuals in America do not have access to lower rent, and decent, affordable homes. Even with easy credit policies it has only grown more and more difficult to afford a home in America. Americans are spending increasingly more of their income on housing. In many cases up to 50% of their income goes towards housing.

In the United States, just because someone works full-time does not mean they can afford a home and all the costs of day-to-day living. Many folks are making daily choices between rent and food, or rent and other necessities. For some in America, tiny homes can provide a suitable housing situation. Tiny homes could be especially suitable for single people or for a small family.

Tiny homes can help expand the rental market and land use density in many places. Building tiny homes in cottage communities with land preserved for open space and farmland could leave land intact for amenities such as food production, natural spaces, wildlife habitat, recreation, and community development.

Tiny house rentals might help alleviate housing shortages while at the same time provide passive income to the homeowners, which is a valuable win/win situation for all parties.

Individuals can make a tremendous difference in the world, and in this case, in housing affordability. There are ways in which one individual, you, can help with solving America's housing crisis.

Your personal participation can help. Volunteer with a program such as Habitat for Humanity. Or it could be as simple as providing one rental unit at an affordable rent. It could even be donating a few hours of your time to help a friend or neighbor construct a home as in the old house-raising days. Perhaps "tiny home raisings" will become a fashionable community service, church and recreational event, patterned after the very successful Habitat for Humanity building program.

Providing tiny homes could be an active part of helping to eliminate critical housing needs. If more people are willing to invest and become a resource to provide affordable housing, it is possible that the goal of solving America's housing problems could be met.

Tiny House FAQ

1. How does the cost of a tiny house compare to the cost of a standard size house?

Tiny houses are much less expensive than larger houses simply because they are smaller. They use less building materials and have less heated and air conditioned space. Consequently, they are less expensive to heat and maintain year after year.

However, tiny houses still need the plumbing, electrical, bath and kitchen fixtures, and appliances such as a stacked washer/dryer, the same as a larger house. So the cost per square foot is higher, but there are fewer square feet so the bottom line is less.

You can save money by doing some of the work yourself. Don't forget that in addition to the house costs, there are the costs of your lot's site development, which would include clearing, roads, well, hook-ups, septic, and landscaping.

2. What is the realistic resale value of a tiny house?

There is precedence that architectural detail, efficient use of space, and contemporary amenities attract not only buyers, but also national media attention. There is a growing backlash to the "McMansionization" of American housing. Smaller-scale homes are more livable, enjoyable and socially more responsible. Every inch is used and nicely finished. For example, in a modest Seattle neighborhood, houses of only 400 to 500 square feet sold right away to single men and women for over $100,000.

3. I don't have a lot of money; can my tiny house be added on to later?

YES! You can design and frame your tiny house so that a future addition can easily be added. For example, you can frame a window to become a door in the future. A roofline can be designed so that it can easily be extended or attached to another roofline. Decks can be bolted in place temporarily so that they can be removed and reinstalled when rooms are added.

4. I need to live on a smaller budget, as I will soon have a fixed income. Will a tiny house help me do this?

Yes, smaller homes are much more efficient to heat and cool than larger homes and can save a lot of dollars on utilities. Most folks don't realize that much of their house simply stores stuff — in heated and cooled space. These stored items are usually things one doesn't really use in their day-to-day life and are things that don't need to be stored in living space.

5. I own a house in town. Can I put a tiny house on that lot and still meet the building codes?

In some cases the answer is probably YES. Many city ordinances and regulations allow for guest cottages and granny units that can be built on an existing lot and tied into the sewer and water connections. Check with your local zoning official to see if a freestanding addition to your home is possible.

6. What about pets in a tiny house?

Pets are part of many people's lifestyles. They bring joy and smiles every day. You can easily install a pet door in your home, and build "cat-walks" or other special places your pets might enjoy.

7. I have bad allergies. Can I have a house that minimizes my allergic reactions?

YES! Many folks don't realize how the materials used in new homes can aggravate allergies. Materials such as carpeting, insulation, and finishes, all give off gases that are toxic. Some studies show indoor air pollution to be five or more times higher than outdoor air pollution. You can search for up-to-date information and the latest building materials to build healthy, hypoallergenic homes on the Internet.

8. How do you move and set a tiny house?

Modular companies move house sections routinely. They have experienced crane and trucks build for the task. You can probably find, and can hire a local one.

9. How do you set a tiny house?

A tiny house can be set on any type of foundation, even on piers. This also allows them to be relatively easily moved. If you relocate and want to take your tiny home with you, just hiring a moving company and a crane.

10. What will my neighbors think about tiny houses?

Resistance sometimes comes from neighbors who are concerned that cottage-style housing will lessen the value of their larger single-family homes. But when up-scale tiny houses are architecturally custom designed and blended into the existing neighborhoods, these tiny houses become attractive assets and increase the value of the homes, and the neighborhood.

Tiny House Glossary

In this glossary, I'll briefly describe some of the most important terms along with other concepts and descriptions of new green building materials. This might help you to begin thinking about your home space in terms specific to smaller spaces. These definitions will help you explain to your design person what your intent is in designing your home the way you want it.

Agroforestry. Land management for the simultaneous production of food crops and trees. Cultivated bamboo groves are considered as agroforestry and produce many wood-like products including flooring, cabinets, furniture, plywood and other products useful in building houses.

Alternative Housing. It seems in America that anything other than a three bedroom, two bath, two-car garage, single family home is considered alternative housing. Small and tiny homes are certainly considered alternative housing in the United States.

Autoclaved Aerated Concrete Blocks (AAC). AAC blocks are made from sand or fly ash (a waste product from the coal combustion). AAC blocks and panels are organic, dimensionally accurate and durable. The cellular structure of the material provides extraordinary thermal lag and sound insulation. They are not recommend for use in below-grade construction or for foundations.

Away Space. A place where you can get away from the main activities of a household or community. Another term often used is "a place of one's own." These rooms or spaces can be an art studio, pout-house, hobby hut, writer's nook, meditation center or hide-away place to relax and regenerate. Many people want bigger houses because they think that will give them a place to themselves. Tiny houses can fill the niche as relatively inexpensive away spaces for that personal privacy.

Bathroom Bucket. Bathroom buckets were widely used before indoor plumbing became common. The "night soil" or human excrement can be used for fertilizing the soil, as it is high in nitrogen.

Sometimes a tiny home is too tiny to have a bathroom. A simple 5-gallon bucket and a toilet seat can be used instead of having to build a regular size bathroom. Often a high carbon material, such as peat moss or sawdust, is placed in the bucket as an absorbent.

In the morning take bucket and flush the urine in the regular toilet. Urine is sterile so it isn't necessarily unsanitary.

Big Houses. Is bigger better? The trend is for bigger and bigger houses that have a lot of square footage. But usually these end up being huge personal storage containers. As a culture, we mistake equating value primarily to square footage. Instead we should equate value with livability, a sense of quality and comfort.

Building Code. The construction requirements for building a house.

Bungalow. Usually one-storied house with a low-pitched roof and surrounded by a wide veranda (deck), or front porch.

Cistern. A receptacle for holding water or other liquids, especially a tank for collecting and storing rainwater.

Codicil House. A smaller house close to a larger house, a co-domicile. Also called granny unit in some locations.

Conservation Subdivision. Subdivisions designed to preserve natural green space and include areas for wildlife habitat, food production and recreation. House lots are often made small in order to leave more open common land that is usually owned and maintained by the homeowner's association.

Cottage Communities. Neighborhoods or subdivisions made up primarily of smaller houses such as cottages and bungalows.

Cowboy or Summer Kitchen. The summer kitchen can still be found on many farms and ranches today. Traditionally, when several farm families got together to harvest each other's crops, the big meal of the day was the "Farmer's Nooning" or noon meal, prepared in an outdoor or field kitchen.

Downsizing. Taking an assessment of the things (stuff) in your life and deciding which items really serve you usefully versus which items are redundant or just clutter. See also stuffology. Downsizing can also mean reducing the size of your living quarters, or reducing the size of your debt and workload.

Fear of Too Smallness. Especially in America we seem to be so attached to so much stuff that we actually develop a phobia or fear of being cramped without enough storage room. Big houses ease that fear of enough space for all our stuff, but at what cost?

Footprint. This is the outline of a house's foundation on the earth.

Feng Shui. The Chinese art of placement. Feng and Shui translate to wind and water. The art of Feng Shui consists in trapping and pooling good life energy (ch'i), and repelling bad energy from a site. It reaches back into the traditional Taoist's philosophy that actions on earth affect the heavens and movements in the heavens act upon the surface of the Earth. As above, so below.

Granny Flat. A small house or apartment around 500 square feet. So named so granny (grandmother) could have her own space but be close by the family. Same as codicil homes. Tiny houses can often qualify as granny units.

Happily Incompatible. To willingly accept one another's differences. To be thankful for each other and the dissimilar qualities. Choosing acceptance rather than anger and resentment when faced with differences in being. Many couples realize they are happily incompatible and choose to live separately.

Human Proportions. See third dimension.

Inappropriately Housed. The state of living in a house that does not properly fit one's lifestyle and needs. A house may be inappropriate for an individual or family due to size, location, finances, accessibility, or any number of reasons.

Lifestyle Homes. Everyone has a slightly different lifestyle that includes hobbies and special things they like to do. By their design and function, homes can reflect the lifestyle of their owners.

Light on Two Sides of Every Room. Two walls with windows have a huge affect on tiny houses. Rooms with light from two walls and with natural light have less glare and better perception of details. Two-sided light lets you read in detail the minute expressions that flash across a person's face, the motion of their hands and thereby understand more clearly. The light on two sides of a room allows people to understand each other. It also gives the room a more spacious and welcoming environment.

McMansions, Mini-mansions & Starter Castles. This is a term referring to the increasing size of the average house in America. Super-sized homes with a lot of square footage, but not much personality. The average size of the American home has grown from roughly 900 square feet with two bedrooms and one bath in the 1950's to over 2,000 square feet in the 2000's. The average millennium houses have three bedrooms, three and a half baths, eat-in kitchen, dining room, home entertainment center, and a two, but often three car garage.

Niche Housing. We are defining niche housing as houses that supply a specialized need and habitat for non-mainstream people.

Park Model. These small homes are technically recreational vehicles, just like motor homes, 5th wheel trailers and travel trailers. However, park models are actually luxury cabins or small homes. They are on wheels and are semi-mobile. They are called park models because they are often found in camp grounds.

Permaculture. Permaculture is derived from permanent agriculture. Bill Mollison defined permaculture in his book by the same name as: "The conscious design and maintenance of agriculturally productive ecosystems which have the diversity, stability, and resilience of natural ecosystems. It is the harmonious integration of landscape and people providing for their food, energy, shelter, and other material and non-material needs in a sustainable way. The philosophy behind permaculture is working with, rather than against nature, of looking at systems in all their functions, rather than asking only one yield of them and allowing systems to demonstrate their own evolutions."

Pods of Space. Pods of space means a small area with its own defined space, personality and special definition.

Pout House. A pout house is a place to go and pout, or let others pout, as such behavior is unpleasant to be around.

Rainwater Harvesting. Collecting, storing, and using rainwater. Usually this is done from roofs and collected in rain barrels, cisterns, ponds and lakes.

Spatial Perception. Spatial: of pertaining to, involving or having the nature of space, and perception: an impression in the mind, insight, intuition or knowledge gained by perceiving. This is the way you feel in one size space compared to another. For example, a house with a cathedral ceiling has a totally different spatial perception than when you are in a smaller room with lower ceilings. In tiny houses sensory spatial perception is more acute. Light seems brighter, sounds are clearer and smells are more easily noticed. Subliminal sensing is easier tuned into and made conscious. Spatial perception can be part of the magic of living in tiny homes because you can notice subtle changes in your environment easier.

Starter Castle. See McMansions and Mini-Mansions.

Stuffology. The study of how stuff, possessions, especially personal and household things, impact and affect our daily lives.

Third Dimension. The third dimension is height, and in building terms relates to heights of ceilings and how those heights relate to human proportions. Vaulted ceilings usually make us feel smaller.

Tithing. In the olden days, tithing was an agricultural term meaning to leave behind 10% of the crop on the fields to fertilize the soils. It also meant saving 10% of the seeds for next year's planting. Modern definition of tithing refers to giving away some amount of money, usually 10%, to charity or humane purposes. Around the 14th century the church defined tithing to mean donating to the clergy. The metaphysical message embedded in tithing is that by giving away money you are acknowledging a prosperity consciousness and that there is enough money to go around. We expanded the definition of tithing to include donating time, items, and service to charitable organizations, beings in need, or to your community.

Tiny House. We define a tiny house as being from around 600 square feet to 1,100 square feet.

Tiny, Tiny House. We define tiny, tiny houses as being from around 300 square feet to 600 square feet.

Unhoused. This is a term we use to describe folks who, for whatever reason, don't have a decent house to call home. This doesn't necessarily mean just impoverished street people. For example, the unhoused could include domestically abused individuals who need a place to stay until their problems are resolved.

Universal Design. The intent of universal design is to make housing usable by more people at little or no extra cost. A universal design component can be used by persons having limited abilities. The Universal Design concept was developed and is promoted by the Center for Universal Design at the North Carolina State University, College of Design. www.design.ncsu.edu.cud.

Visit-ability. Providing universal access to those who may wish to visit you. Offering a comfortable passage into one's home. The ability to easily accommodate all people, including those with disabilities, by enabling easy and graceful access into a building.

Voluntary Simplicity. "Voluntary", from one's free will or initiative and simplicity: the state or quality of being simple; absence of complexity. To live a voluntarily simple life is to be conscious of your actions, thoughts, and being and to strive for simplicity however you might define that for yourself. This includes the philosophy of living more purposefully and minimizing distractions. For example, downsizing by decreasing the number of items you own might save you time and money.

*****

Tiny House Basics: A Complete Introduction

What Are Tiny Houses?

Even though average home sizes in the United States have been growing, many people are discovering that they can live in a lot less room. Many times, they even find themselves living much happier, fulfilling lives with less space. These people are redefining the dream of Americans and living sustainably. Tiny houses can be up to 500 square feet in size, but many are dramatically smaller.

Typical Features

"Small" is the operative word in a tiny house. A typical tiny home may be 100-200 square feet, with a small kitchen – often galley style, as that is quite space-efficient. The bathroom is – yes, small – with a commode and shower. Sleeping areas are also included, of course, though they are usually a lofted space. The main living area is sometimes a bit larger than the other parts of the house.

Built-ins are often used to increase the usable space of a tiny house. Bookshelves, desks and wardrobes or dressers can be built-in, to offer more storage space. Many builders use reclaimed wood and other materials, to make their imprint on the environment smaller.

Why So Tiny?

"Tiny Housers", as they are sometimes known, understand that getting rid of excess "stuff" can free up your energy, time and money, in order that you may focus on what is truly important to you. Keeping a simple lifestyle and receiving lower utility bills allows these homeowners to spend more time working on projects and traveling.

People who live in tiny houses also connect with the natural world in a way that is more personal. Smaller houses are more easily integrated into a natural area than are typical styles of American homes.

Media Coverage

Tiny houses are becoming more popular as they are featured in media coverage. Many people want to own their own homes, but cannot afford to, in the world of conventional homes. There are also tiny houses on wheels, which allow you to literally "take it all with you" when you move.

Tiny House Safety

Since many of the original tiny houses were developed in the minds of non-professional builders, it was necessary to ensure that these houses would be built in a safe manner. Even amateur builders can access blueprints and safety information online, so that their homes will be safe places in which to live.

Zoning

People who wish to build tiny houses sometimes run into roadblocks in the form of zoning laws. Most zoning regulations have a specified minimum number of square feet for new construction.

Even if you are building a house on wheels, you likely will not be able to park it in your driveway, since this would fall under the zoning rules against camping.

The Tiny House Philosophy

Living in a small house often leaves no mortgage payments, which means you can be relatively free of debt. You can attend DIY Tiny House workshops, and tiny houses are a valuable way to attack the problem of people not being able to afford housing.

True Tiny Housers live in their diminutive homes full-time. Others use them for guest homes, offices or vacation cottages. Builders must be able to purchase or rent land for their houses, in additional to finding a location that will allow this type of house. Conventional bank loans are usually not available, since tiny houses are not considered traditional assets.

In tiny houses, every square inch is utilized. They blend functionality with aesthetics. Skylights and windows bring in natural light, to avoid sole dependence on utilities. You may wish to install solar panels, so that you can live more fully off the grid, and lower your utility bills to next to nothing.

Tiny houses are unlike any other type of living – unless you have lived in a trailer for months on end. They are usually much smaller even than mobile homes. Tiny houses are certainly not for everyone, but minimalists may be quite content with a smaller house and smaller bills. This book will give you a beginner's overview to what Tiny Houses are, who lives in them, and how the Tiny House lifestyle can benefit you, in more ways than you could even imagine…So, let's get to it!

Chapter 1 - Different Types of Tiny Houses

Tiny homes may all be small, but that's one of the few things they have in common. The truth is that there are almost as many different types of tiny houses as there are people looking to live in one. Builders may construct these homes from many different resources, used in various ways. Floor plans, too, are becoming ever more unique and innovative. In this chapter, we will describe the various materials and methods used to build tiny houses.

Pre-Manufactured Tiny Houses

Building a conventional house can be very expensive, especially if you design the home yourself and loaded with all the features you want. Many people will never have a house built to their specifications. Selecting a prefabricated wooden house will help in keeping your costs down, but it still may be out of reach for many homebuyers. It is certainly a much more attainable goal when you start looking at tiny houses.

Materials prices are going up without pause, and banks are starting to loan money more stingily since the economy is well on its way to recovery. The smartest solution, if you want everything done your way, to truly live in your dream house, may be to go small.

How Small Are Pre-Manufactured Tiny Houses?

Prefabricated tiny houses are becoming more popular. Getting back to nature and reducing their carbon footprint is presenting an attractive solution for some homebuyers. The smallest of tiny houses built from plans is usually about 100 square feet. By comparison, a "studio" apartment with no bedroom is about 300-450 square feet.

In a world where lending rates are trending upward, tiny homes appeal to more and more homebuyers. You can be the king or queen of your castle without a mortgage, if your "castle" is a tiny house.

Advantages to tiny houses on your wallet are many, even though living "small" will mean making many changes in your expectations and in the way you live. However, you will have smaller utility bills, smaller property tax bills and your home can be set up on your lot in much less time than it takes to build a conventional wood-frame or brick house. Your home can be quite energy-efficient, and you can maximize your investment.

Tiny House Blueprints

Modern tiny houses come in many styles, configurations, materials, and many are built on wheels. Builders make them with new materials or reclaimed materials from other homes and sources, to lower the cost.

Even in tiny house blueprints, you may have a functional-sized kitchen, with traditional sized appliances, and plenty of room for storage. Tiny house blueprints may include furnishings that double as places for storage, and a fully functional bathroom, although you may need to adjust to a composting toilet rather than a flush toilet, in some models.

A 200 square foot house can feel spacious and open, with taller ceilings than you would expect. Some have 11-foot ceilings, and you can often add amenities you wouldn't know were available in these diminutive homes. Even blueprints for houses that are small enough to be legally trucked on roads can allow plenty of living room.

Tiny home plans are ready to build, and they are professionally drawn and engineered. Architects design many tiny home building plans for the novice builder, and they can be assembled using basic techniques and innovative, new engineering.

Basic Features in Tiny Home Blueprints

Designers offer basic features in blueprints for some tiny houses, including:

- A full sized kitchen with conventional sized appliances
- Lounge or guest loft
- Propane heat sources
- Standard bathroom sink
- Composting toilet for off-grid homes
- Complete plans for off-grid and on-grid placement

A typical tiny house blueprint has specifications that include:

- 200+ square feet of living space on main floor with 110 square foot lofts
- Insulation in roof is about R-25 and in walls, R-17

Non-Traditional Tiny Houses

Workers may not pre-fabricate or build tiny houses with conventional materials. This next section covers some of the more unique ways you can build a tiny house.

Shipping Container Homes

You've seen shipping containers before, although you may not have ever thought about using them to build a home. Transport companies use them on ships and trains, and many of them are left sitting empty at ports on both coasts of the United States. These can be recycled into eco-friendly, stylish housing that is very cost-efficient to build, as compared to conventional construction.

How Shipping Container Tiny Homes Have Evolved

People originally used cargo containers for emergency housing. Wealthy, green homeowners have used them for vacation homes. Today, they are less fringe homes and are more in the mainstream of tiny houses.

Corrugated steel storage containers can be used for more than simple houses. Workers clean and paint the containers – they are often treated with chemicals when built– and they may be used for single-family homes, senior housing and even apartment homes. Depending on the size needed, various numbers of units are used in the construction of each building.

What Is the Worth of Storage Container Homes?

Viewed from outside, shipping container homes often range from 150 to over 3,000 square feet. Obviously, the latter are not tiny houses. They may appear similar to tract homes, and the boxes are covered with skins (special finishes) and enhanced by the addition of large windows and custom paint.

Inside, storage container homes may have bamboo or other elegant flooring and appliances that offer you the best of energy-efficiency. Insulation is important, since the metal can get quite cold in winter and very hot in the summer.

Shipping Container Tiny Houses Become More Viable

Tiny homes made from shipping containers do take some preparation, but their average cost to convert into homes is about $85-$200 per square foot, as compared with the $250+ per square foot cost for traditional homes.

Architects state that container houses are at least 20% cheaper to construct than houses built using traditional methods. You can build very basic homes for less than $100 per square foot.

How to Think Inside the Box

Since the United States imports more than we export, there are hundreds of thousands of empty containers sitting empty in port cities. Builders can purchase these containers for low prices, usually between $1,000 and $2,500. The price depends on the condition, location and size.

With the prices for steel and lumber rising, shipping containers are a virtual bargain, and their standard height is 9.5 feet, which gives them clearance, so they don't look or feel like storage sheds.

Shipping container homes are easier to assemble at the building site than framed houses. This speeds up construction, which lowers your cost. They are quite sturdy, and builders use them for housing in earthquake and hurricane-prone areas.

The companies that retrofit shipping containers into "blocks", or building units, are often located in port cities. Some blueprints contain three to five units for a typical single-family home, but tiny houses make use of fewer containers per home.

Some retrofitters of tiny storage container houses use the plywood floors found in the existing containers. If these floors or the containers themselves were treated with chemicals for use at sea, they will need to be painted or treated to ensure that they are safe for occupancy.

Builders can use shipping containers as the building blocks for many tiny house plans, with polished floors and large glass windows. The main living area is usually the largest room in the house, with bedrooms and bathrooms generally small. As far as building codes, your ability to get any type of tiny house approved, including storage container housing, depends on the codes in your area. Some cities and counties are open to the new ideas, and some are not.

Clean and Green

Some forward-looking cities are already embracing the idea of storage containers used for tiny houses, because it makes sense in a green way, and it creates affordable housing. These units typically go to waste, and putting them to use makes your home quite eco-friendly. Retrofitting storage containers into homes or office buildings takes about 5% of the amount of energy needed to convert the same units into scrap metal. With such an abundance of recycled building materials, it makes good sense to use containers in tiny house construction.

We will probably not see "cities" of storage container homes in the United States, due to the various building codes in place. In addition, even though you might think that this building idea is "cool", many Americans prefer traditional homes.

One way this is overcome is by putting different materials on the containers, to change the way they look. Adding glass, stucco and brick is more expensive, but these homes may be more palatable for those who enforce local building codes.

In urban areas, where old industrial buildings are recycled into living space in the form of lofts, storage container tiny houses may have more appeal. One company that specializes in retrofitting storage containers into tiny houses and other homes had a waiting list of 10,000 potential customers when their website went online a number of years ago.

School Bus Tiny Houses

If you are not looking forward to signing reams of paperwork to buy a conventional house in a neighborhood full of similar conventional homes, maybe you're one of the people who might consider building or living in a tiny home made from a school bus.

Depending on location, school bus homes may be equipped with wood stoves, which can keep this small area warm and toasty on the coldest nights. If it gets a bit hot, just open a window and natural ventilation will take care of it.

Designers may line with timber any retrofitted school buses made into tiny houses, for a natural look. They have the same types of shelving commonly used on boats, so that things stored on the shelves do not move around too much, if you travel in your tiny home. You can even get fully functional plumbing in a school bus house. Old buses are not very fuel-efficient, but no one said that you have to drive it, once you find a place where you'd like to live.

The New "Mobile Home" Tiny House

If you're tired of shopping for homes that all look alike, inside and out, maybe a school bus is just the thing for you. Old buses are usually not expensive, and if you purchase them and retrofit them yourself, you can design them any way you like. An old school bus has room for a kitchen, sleeping area and bathroom. You can repurpose wood from older buildings for the floors.

One well-known tiny house builder is a college student who goes by the name "Hank" in his blog. He was tired of designing buildings for rich clients he would never meet, in architecture classes. For his Masters project, he bought an old school bus and converted it into a tiny house.

He admits it isn't the most original idea, but he liked the concept of converting old, unused vehicles into affordable, flexible homes. In fact, the bus and all its improvements cost less than one semester of his schooling.

Hank also wanted to demonstrate the importance of making affordable housing, as opposed to spending hours drawing up plans that might never be used. Even if those plans were used, contractors would build them with top of the line materials, which is not very eco-friendly at all.

Hank and his friends designed and built the school bus tiny house in less than four months, in time for it to count for Hank's final project. The design allows versatility in the center area, which can be used with a queen-sized bed, or for other purposes. The tiny bus house can sleep six people. Hank left the windows unblocked to allow for better natural light during the day. He converted two emergency hatches into skylights.

Plans for the Future

This innovative former architecture student wanted to generate more discussion about tiny houses and living in these smaller spaces. The tiny "home bus" idea may be converted to run on a biofuel, to make it more eco-friendly.

Other Innovative Tiny Home Ideas

SIP (Structural Insulated Panels) Tiny Homes

In Louisiana, they call their seasons "winter, almost summer, summer and still summer". This area has many kinds of moisture problems, even in the winter months. Before electricity was readily available, architects designed homes to manage moisture naturally. They were un-insulated, which allowed buildings to leak air. This was the idea: that hot air would rise and escape.

Actually, though, most houses just stayed the same temperature as the outside air, which could be quite hot in the summer months. Today, most homes are air-conditioned, and are battling with the environment nearly every day.

Those are just two examples of dealing with moisture. However, the most effective design provides natural airflow when the outside air is comfortable, and a well-sealed shell, without leaks, when you need air conditioning.

There is plenty of information available on the best ways to construct an energy-efficient, well-insulated tiny house. The elements required for energy-efficient buildings are:

- A water barrier that sheds water
- Insulation, to slow heat transfer
- An air barrier, to allow moisture through and prevent air penetration
- A vapor barrier, to prevent air and moisture from traveling through

These individual elements may consist of separate layers, or one layer, to provide multiple elements. Builders can solve all of the moisture and vapor issues and air leaks by the use of SIP panels for tiny houses

What Are SIP Houses?

If you have noticed the lumber in some older homes tends to bend and bow, you may appreciate building a home with Structural Insulated Panels. SIP walls are square, straight and plumb. A continuous wood surface is a sound base for all interior and exterior finishes.

Your SIP panel home may be one of the most clean, comfortable and quiet structures you can own. SIP panels have insulation built in, leaving few thermal breaks, and this greatly reduces moisture and air penetration.

SIP panels are straighter and stronger, when it comes to using them for your tiny house. They will begin paying you back with lower cooling and heating costs as soon as you move into your home. Contractors install the panels, rather than building them on-site, ensuring that the walls are plumb and straight. It is also a time-saver, so your labor hours will be lower.

The factory installs electrical chases in SIP foam layers, which eliminates the time and expense of drilling holes on-site. SIP panels are plumb and flat, so your drywall contractor can complete the work more quickly. Interior finishes are easier to install, since SIP panels have a continuous surface on which to attach cabinetry, moldings and floorings. There is no need for your installer to search for studs, since nails can penetrate properly anywhere on the SIP panel.

Contractors can easily build airtight structures with SIPs, since every surface is solid. Only one joint will need to be sealed. SIP tiny houses, by design, allow hot air to rise. Gable roofs allow workers to position windows high enough to provide passive vents.

Combining basic knowledge of cohabitating with the environment and adding modern technology allows the building of SIP tiny houses that are comfortable, and that minimize the need for air conditioning.

Teardrop Houses, also called E-Dens

These mini-cabins are unique, even when it comes to the world of tiny houses. The company that started these mini-cabins originally designed them for camping, but they come with a lovely interior, lots of storage space and a king sized bunk bed. The ceiling-placed window brings in natural light and any breeze that is passing by.

The covered front porch of an E-Den has a section of canvas that opens, allowing you to ventilate an on-porch barbeque unit. The windows are double-glazed and builders fully insulate every part of the tiny house. The inside measurements are a less-than-generous 11' x 6'9" and the inside height is 6'9". That is actually quite adequate, unless you're a professional basketball player. The outside dimensions are 14' x 8' x 9' high. The deck has plenty of room, at 7' x 14'.

These E-Dens are marketed to property owners, for rental to campers. However, if you want your own getaway home and you have a lake or wooded lot, why rent a mini-cabin when you can buy one? Your friends will thank you every summer.

Tiny Pallet Houses

Pallets are versatile materials for tiny houses, from their use as cladding and interior walls, to entire houses built from pallets. Four billion pallets are in use today, and used pallets can be economical or even free to obtain.

Tiny pallet houses are as strong as conventionally framed homes, according to many residential homebuilders. In tiny houses, the pallets do not need to be staggered, as they do in larger homes. It is best to use pallets that are all the same size, or as close as you can get.

Once the foundation type is determined, cleats are secured and the pallets are slipped over the concrete blocks. Workers secure them with screws, and clamp each pallet together using C-clamps. Skilled workers will fasten pallets together with carriage bolts or screws, with the corners butted together. They will repeat this process along the foundation perimeter.

Some pallets are heat-treated and some are not. Most tiny house builders use only heat-treated pallets in their homes. They use all-natural materials to insulate tiny pallet houses, including straw clay. Then they add adobe plaster inside and out, for thermal mass and insulation.

Tiny Hobbit Houses

Hobbit houses are usually quite natural in appearance. The builders work with respect for the environment, and give homeowners a chance to live in harmony with nature. Depending on the builder, the only basic tools needed are a chisel, a hammer and a chainsaw. Some builders of tiny hobbit houses have no prior experience in home construction, but it is a good idea to have someone help you with the plans and the major work. Builders may dig these houses into hillsides for shelter and for low visual impact. When the ground is leveled, the mud and stone can be used for foundations and retaining walls.

Builders sometimes frame tiny hobbit houses with spare wood from the area, and the roof rafters are aesthetic and structurally sound. Straw bales are included in the roof, walls and floor, for ease of building and for effective insulation.

Plastic sheeting and a turf or mud roof are used for ease of care and low impact on the environment. Using lime plaster on the walls creates a breathable wall and, compared to cement, it costs less energy to manufacture. Workers make the fittings and floors from reclaimed scrap wood. Wood burners are often installed for heat, if the wood is locally plentiful. The flue for the burner goes through a lump in the plaster and stone, to allow it to retain heat and slowly release it.

Skylights in a tiny hobbit house let in natural light. Water can be sourced from a nearby spring and solar panels provide electricity for lighting, computing and music. The roof collects water in a pond for the garden, and using a compost toilet allows off the grid use.

As you can see, there are many types of tiny houses from which to make your choice. Depending on the materials available in your area, you can choose those that will make your home more cost-effective to build and to maintain.

Chapter 2 - Pros and Cons of Tiny Houses

Just as with any homes, tiny houses have their positive and negative aspects. When you weigh them all, you will generally find that the advantages outweigh the disadvantages, but they are all important for you to know going in.

Advantages of Tiny Houses

Lower Initial Costs

Tiny houses simplify your life. The initial cost is much less than that for building a conventional home. Since they are smaller, fewer materials are needed, and less labor is required. The price per square foot, not counting appliances, is a good deal less than traditional homes. Once you add in all the fixtures and appliances, the cost per square foot will sometimes be a bit higher – but you will only have a fraction of the square footage that you do with a typical-sized framed house.

Unlike conventional homes, you won't have space that you may feel needs to be filled with knick-knacks or other items. You will only be buying what you need. You will be able to afford better furniture, since fewer pieces are required. Decorating is easier and more basic when your environment is smaller.

Many young people cannot afford conventional homes. They will probably be able to save money or get a smaller loan for tiny houses, though. The revolution also appeals to people who are retiring, and looking to downsize their expenses and their lifestyle.

You won't have to pay lot rent every month, as you do with mobile or modular homes. You can purchase your lot.

Most tiny houses have everything you need to live. You'll have a living room, a kitchen, a bathroom and sleeping areas. Not everyone is cut out for tiny house living, but if you seek simplicity in your life, a tiny house may be the way to go.

Lower Energy Consumption

Tiny houses obviously need a lot less energy when you are cooling and heating them, since the interior is so much smaller than other houses. If you have a tiny house with wheels, you can move your house to a shadier spot in the summer, and into a sunny area in the winter. You will probably use a smaller water heater and refrigerator in a tiny house, too, which will save on energy costs. If you use wind turbines, wood stoves, solar panels and composting toilets, you will save even more. You can even go off the grid and supply all your own power.

In an interesting twist, it will also take less personal energy to maintain a tiny house. You won't spend nearly as much time cleaning as you would with a conventional house.

Less Land and Upkeep Costs

Tiny houses do not require as much land as conventional houses. You will need to find a lot in an area that does not have size restrictions, and on which you will be allowed to build your tiny house. Land outside of cities is cheaper for you to buy, and the taxes are lower. You'll spend less time cutting grass, and you will still have room for a garden.

More Disposable Income

Because you spend less on a lot, your home, its furnishings, utilities and property taxes, you will have more of your income left for discretionary spending. When you own a home, a great majority of your expenses are house-related. With less "house" comes less money spent. You slash your living expenses when you own and live in a tiny house.

You may be able to save for your tiny house and build it without having to incur much debt. Tiny houses move people out of asphyxiating mortgages or rentals and into their own homes. You will probably not be able to get a conventional mortgage loan from a bank or mortgage company to finance your tiny house, but you can likely still get a bank loan, just as you would if you bought a motor home.

Big houses often come with huge mortgages. If that's not what you want, you may not need any loan at all for a tiny house, if you save your money to pay for it. If you don't have a mortgage, you won't be stressed, wondering how your family can make the house payments in times of job loss or other financial hardship.

Less Consumption of Water

If you have a smaller hot water heater and shower than you have in a traditional home, you will probably take shorter showers.

Using less water is a positive thing for your wallet, as well as for the environment.

Less Food on Hand

Since your pantry is so much smaller than that of a conventional house, you won't keep as much food in your house. You will likely have a garden too, so some of your meals will be coming from fresh foods that you grow yourself. Not only will your food bills be lower, but your weight may be lower, too, since you will be eating healthy foods.

Less Costly Repairs

Since there is less of everything in a tiny house – smaller roof, rooms, exterior – any repairs or improvements will generally cost less. This is due to a reduction in not only materials, but time, as well.

Lower Insurance Costs

Tiny houses are cheaper to insure, because there is less to insure. You will do well with smaller insurance premiums, leaving more money for other things. If you do have a claim for damage to your home, it will probably be smaller than a similar impact on a larger, conventional home.

Lower Taxes

Your land value and that of your tiny house is less than the larger lots and conventional homes most people have. This means that you will pay less in taxes, and you can put your money saved away for college for the children, or for retirement, vacations or investments.

Less Interest on Your Home Loan

When you buy a conventional house, your first payments go mainly toward interest, with just small amounts going toward the principle. When you buy a tiny house, you may pay cash for it, or pay it off in a much shorter period of time. The interest saved will be a substantial amount.

More Efficiency

Tiny houses are undeniably efficient. When builders design tiny houses, they eliminate unnecessary and inefficient space. Tiny houses allow you to use every bit of space within them. They are one type of future homes, where you can live in comfort, without debt, and still have everything you need. Tiny Housers will tell you that you only live in one room of your home at any given time. If you have room for all your needs, then you don't need any more.

More Freedom

When you choose life in a tiny house, you will free up resources, time and money. You'll also be saving the Earth. When you spend a lot on mortgage payments on conventional homes, you will have less available for taking time off and heading away for vacations.

If you are concerned about the world around you, and leaving the environment in good shape for the next generation, tiny houses allow you to do this, as well. You use fewer natural resources and you free up time.

Freedom to Move

If you're like most people, you probably hate moving. With tiny houses on wheels, all you need to do is drive to your destination in your house. Tiny homes on truck chassis' make moving easy. Think of the exciting possibilities.

You can take a better job somewhere else and take your house with you. You will avoid the hassle of selling your old house and purchasing another in your new work area. You won't ever have to rent a moving truck or pay a moving company.

You can even stay "with" friends or family for a long period of time without cramping their style. You may leave your lot in advance of anticipated hurricanes or other natural disasters like mudslides or wildfires. You won't have hotel bills on your road trips. You can go anywhere you want on vacation and take your vacation home with you.

A New Credo

Your tiny home will include suitable rooms for living, but no space wasted on hallways. The materials used can be salvaged, and solar panels will allow you to potentially live off the grid. Heaters that use wood are eco-friendly, since there is dead wood in most areas. Air conditioning, which is required in so many areas in the summer, can be solar powered.

You may need to work at getting out of the consumer culture. Many of us are socialized to buy when we are raised. You will think purchases through with a tiny house, if for no other reason than a lack of space for any "junk" you might find at yard sales or flea markets.

Disadvantages of Tiny Home Living

No home or way of life is completely free of impracticalities. Tiny houses do have their drawbacks, although their positive aspects largely outweigh them.

Living on the Cheap

The same thing that is a positive can also be a negative. People may look on you as they do on extreme coupon cutters and other savers of money. You may be compared to people who live in mobile homes, even though the homes and lots are different for tiny houses.

For many people, bigger will always be better. Even if that's not your credo, it is for many others. People may see you as a transient instead of a homeowner.

Lack of Space

You may miss some of the things you used to have in your conventional home. A conventional washer, a dryer, a flush toilet or a full-sized refrigerator may be things you decide you cannot live without. You can always go back to conventional home ownership, or renting.

You may not have enough room in a tiny house for a home office. If you normally work from home and you build or buy a tiny house, you may need to allocate room for designing, working and filing.

Downsizing Isn't Always Easy

Depending on the location of your tiny house, you may not reside on easily accessible roads. A loft is quite useful for young families, but not so much for retirees. Of course, retirees can always build a tiny house with a sleeping area on the main level.

Many local area government officials are unfamiliar with tiny houses as they fit into building codes. If you have a tiny house on wheels, you are sure to be able to find someplace to park it, but it may not be in the location of your dreams. Scout out your lot before you buy or build a tiny house.

Some people have problems with confined spaces. For them, tiny houses may not be a good fit. If you find a natural lot on which to build or park, you can always extend your living space outdoors, at least when weather allows.

More Human Energy May Be Needed for Building

Tiny houses take a lot of energy and time to build, if you're doing the work yourself. Of course, you can counter this by paying to have your tiny house built, or buy purchasing a prefabricated tiny home.

The Attention Isn't always Positive

Your tiny house will get lot of attention, and it won't always be positive attention. Many people will stop and stare. You will undoubtedly be able to share your ideas with many of these people; most people are simply curious. However, when you want your peace and quiet, gawkers can be annoying. Of course, if you build or park in a natural area, off the beaten trail, you won't have many gawkers.

Works in Progress

Many aspects of tiny houses are works in progress. Things will break, just as they do on conventional homes. Water does not come without limits, and you'll need to be acutely aware that every action may bring on a negative reaction. Garbage disposals will be a thing of the past, but this also teaches you and your children not to waste things.

Interior Choices

Consider your flooring before you get your mind set on a certain type. Dark floors make tiny houses look smaller, and they are harder to keep visibly clean, especially if you have pets. Laying rugs down is a good way to make cleaning easier, if you like dark flooring.

Tiny Houses versus Apartments

Many people hate throwing money away on rent. While you may love your tiny house, a part of you may long for the months you may have spent renting at some time in your life. Your landlord maintained your appliances for you, as well as the roof and the lawn. Granted, tiny houses do not have large lawns, anyway, and much of your lot space may be used for gardening.

Composting Toilets

This is perhaps one of the most-often mentioned disadvantages of tiny house living. Composting does involve carrying buckets of... well, you know... out to a larger bucket somewhere a little ways away from your tiny house, so it can ferment and be used eventually as garden fertilizer.

These are just inconveniences, really. In your conventional home or apartment, you can ignore some of the little things you will have to do if you live in a tiny house. It is overall a small price to pay for the freedom from expenses you have, when you are living in a tiny house.

You're probably quite accustomed to everything being available whenever and wherever you need it. It's helpful to love the land more than convenience, if you want to live in a tiny house.

Putting the Positives and Negatives Together: How Several Families Did It

Now that we have explored some of the individual advantages and disadvantages of building or buying a tiny home, let's look at how several families put their tiny house dreams together, one piece at a time.

Self-sufficiency and gardening, surviving and raising animals is natural for people who grew up in homesteading families. Building and living in a tiny house is a logical extension of this ethic. People raised in this way may try to exist in city life but their heart and soul will call them back to nature. It's especially difficult for homesteaders to suddenly be faced with all the bills that come with city life.

A Wake-Up Call

Alexander had a wake-up call when he was 35 years old. He realized that what he really wanted was a simple house and to eliminate his dependence on the system. He wanted to live sustainably and pursue his dreams.

Living in a tiny house is an excellent way to reduce your carbon footprint, simplify life and save money.

So, Alexander built his house. In fact, he built a very small house – 14 x 14 to be exact. He built a wind and solar powered tiny cabin, off the grid, with a living room, kitchen and bathroom downstairs and an office and bedroom upstairs. The total cost was only $2,000, before the addition of recycled windows and doors, a solar system and a front porch.

Alexander was an avid outdoorsman, and didn't need a lot of interior space. He is, however, a builder, author and videographer, so he needed some modern amenities. These included an indoor toilet, modern shower, electric lights, a cell phone and Internet access. He has them. He says that his tiny house is cheap to cool and heat, mortgage-free and easy to clean, with no utility bills.

Alexander enjoys having the freedom to pursue his dreams. The money he earns stays in his pocket and it can be used for helping his family, saving for retirement and for vacations. He has this freedom because he lives off the grid.

Alexander is one of many new tiny housers. There are more and more people discovering tiny houses. They have even been tested as homelessness solutions. Part of the tiny house movement takes the freedom, simplicity and sustainability of tiny houses one level higher by building them off the grid

Speaking with tiny housers who have gone off-grid, you will learn about their challenges and how they handle everyday, practical matters like electricity, water and sewage. You will learn what you should know about off the grid life and the benefits of combining off the grid life with living tiny.

Benefits and Legalities

Living off the grid in a tiny house is an excellent way to reduce your carbon footprint, while you save money. Your bills for energy and water can be zero, once you have paid for the solar equipment and your well and septic. This allows you to simplify life, and concentrate on what truly matters.

It's worth a thought, at least. People were thriving and surviving long before we had electricity, and if you can do things for yourself, you still can live in a simple way.

One of the benefits of living in a tiny house is that money is freed up, as is energy and time, which you might otherwise spend on home maintenance and mortgage or rent payments. You can use that time for spending time with your family and friends, starting a business or working on unique creative projects. You will also have time to work on hobbies that you enjoy.

The most obvious challenge to tiny house life is the amount of interior space. To counter that, though, you and your family will spend more time out of doors, thinking about what matters most and simplifying your possessions.

Some of the challenges that come with tiny houses are less palatable. Hauling water is difficult and heavy work, and emptying the composting toilet is not an enjoyable experience. However, the homeowners take on these tasks, so that they not only save money, but they understand how much water they consume, so they can conserve, where necessary.

Beating the Building Code Issues

Alexander says that one of his most frustrating challenges was the burdensome building code issue. He faced some initial interference from neighbors. He recalls the need for securing a water supply adequate to his needs. He lives in a rural area, too, so he needed to face isolation and being able to make money in the rural economy.

Nearly everyone who has built a tiny house talks about the importance of speaking with local authorities. The regulations are different in various states, counties and towns. Before you extrapolate long-term plans, call the local planning commission.

In some towns with building restrictions, rules apply only if your neighbors report you. Speak with them and get to know them.

Explain your motivation for choosing the tiny house lifestyle, and create allies of neighbors.

As a rule, the closer you will be living to a city, the more rules you may run into. Due to this issue, many people who live in tiny houses off the grid choose to do so in rural areas. Some of the states that are most friendly to off the grid life include Missouri, Arkansas, Wyoming, Alaska, Oklahoma and Colorado.

Taking Your Tiny House Off Grid

There's a direct relationship between tiny houses and off the grid living. Having a life with less stuff and more experiences is a big driver of the tiny house movement. Going off the grid allows tiny house dwellers to take that simplicity even further.

Part of the tiny home movement is that there is no cookie-cutter solution for all the people who want to build tiny houses. Everyone has access to different resources, and they can help you to go off grid, if that is what you want. Since smaller houses require less energy already, they are a natural match for off grid power solutions.

People who want to live in tiny houses don't all build their own, but many do. This gives them a better understanding of the way utilities work in their home, which helps them to determine the best ways to go off the grid. Tiny housers usually appreciate being environmentally sustainable and self-sufficient. It is easier to live off grid in a small house, as compared to a conventional home.

Many tiny houses are built on wheels, to get around building codes, and they don't have access to septic systems and other utilities. Off grid utilities can be used even if you park your tiny house in a location that does have access to traditional utilities.

How Much Does Off Grid Life Cost?

There is no one answer to what it will cost to live off the grid. It depends on your location and whether you build or buy your house. Other factors are how you heat the house, how much is spent on power sources for going off grid and how simple the house will be. There isn't just one way to live simply, or to live off the grid.

Working with companies that specialize in alternative power sources, you can build the exact system you want for your tiny house. Your plans will include a number of solar panels – the number and size are dependent on the size of your tiny house and what you will be powering with solar energy.

A charge controller is also needed for your solar system, as are AGM batteries. Solar power is direct current, so an inverter is required, to convert that DC to AC current. A grid water filter is also helpful for tiny housers in rural areas.

Your Expenses Will Be Offset by Benefits

If your electricity bill is $0 per month, and that takes care of electricity, water and heat, you are truly an off the grid household. You may incur other costs like repairs, but paying zero for your utilities will offset those expenses, with money to spare. You will still likely have bills for cell phones and Internet access.

The costs for living tiny depend on many things, including where you live. If you have your house parked or built in a location where you can go off the grid, you may just need to purchase a small sized propane tank every few months for your heat. Water may be purchased as well, or bartered for, until you have a well dug. Some tiny houses do cost more to build, but including just the essentials will mean a smaller price tag.

The costs you incur may be lower if you are a minimalist and simply use lanterns and candles for light and propane or wood stoves for your heat. Alternatively, you might decide to build a green, high-tech tiny house, in the model of the newest sustainability guidelines. These homes are more expensive to build, but they are very economical, once completed. You can even remodel older homes to be used off the grid. Many people actually spend more on their solar system than they do on the house, but this, of course, will eventually pay for itself. There is something alluring about not being a slave to the rates of local utility companies.

What Are the Best Electricity Options?

One option for people who really want to go off the grid is going without. 25% of the homes in the world are not connected to the electrical grid. Of course, some of those homeowners have no choice, if they live on the Serengeti, for example.

If you are comfortable doing things by hand, and not watching TV, you can survive and even thrive without electricity. If you don't want to fully go without electricity, solar can be an affordable option. At about $1 per watt, an expansive power system can be purchased for less than $5,000. Contrary to popular belief, solar can also work in snowy areas and cloudy conditions, albeit not as efficiently.

Wind energy is an option that is becoming more popular, but the prices for wind turbines can be quite high. In addition, they only work when the wind is blowing. If your building site has access to a stream or river, you can even use hydropower to generate some of the electricity you need.

Do Your Research before You Build

People who have built tiny homes for themselves or others stress that you need to do your research before you invest time, energy and money in a tiny house, and before you go off the grid. An energy meter will calculate what your needs are. Efficient appliances are a must, and you also have choices in appliances that don't use power. This is why off grid houses use propane heat, wood stoves, fans, alternate power refrigerators and passive cooling to make them more efficient. After you eliminate the appliances that gobble up energy, you'll only need a smaller solar system for the rest of your house.

Alexander uses a 580-watt solar system and a 400-watt wind turbine in his tiny house, along with propane for heat and cooking.

He also has a wood stove, for backup. He passively cools his house with trees, overhangs, porches and fans, and refrigerates with a converted freezer that runs on solar power.

Getting Water Is Basic

Finding a good source for water is something you must research and accomplish before you pay money for land or agree to rent land from the owner. If you are in a rural area, you will want a well that is professionally drilled. You can use shallow wells or rainwater catchment for gardening, but they will not provide enough water for all your needs.

An Artesian well is helpful for off the grid homeowners. Alexander uses rainwater to help in supplementing the household water supply, but it has to be filtered and then treated if you will be using it for cooking or drinking. Rainwater is suitable, however, for flushing toilets and washing clothes. If you're lucky, you may find land with a running spring on it. Conservation is still important.

An average household in the United States uses more than 200 gallons of water per day. This depends on how many people live in the house. In a tiny house, two people may use a total of only five gallons per day, not counting water for drinking. Tiny house owners use air pressurized shower sprayers that only hold two gallons of hot water, which has been enough to help them stay clean and comfortable.

The Ups and Downs of Toilets in Tiny Homes

Outhouses certainly work for toileting purposes, but their smell is a drawback, as is their outdoors location, if it's raining or snowing. Composting toilets allow for indoor use, and they are as comfortable as a regular toilet. You might also look into leach ponds or septic tanks for your waste disposal.

Some tiny housers use sawdust composting toilets, which are supposedly easy to manage. You can purchase a commercial compost system, but these tend to be pricey. Our house-building friend Alexander actually designed and then built a composting toilet that is solar enhanced. It keeps the microbes at higher temperatures, so they compost waste more quickly.

If gray water is eliminated from the tank, according to Alexander, you won't need a leach field. There won't be anything left over except some composted, dry materials when the composting process is complete. You can find plans for toilets and composting systems in off the grid books, or do an online search.

Other Issues – Internet Access, Garbage, Recycling and Snail Mail

If you live off the grid, how will you handle garbage, recycling, Internet access and US mail? Local dumps are usually used for garbage disposal and recycling. For US mail, you can rent a PO box or set up a mailbox at the local UPS store. Alternately, you may simply mount a mailbox on a post and set it up by the road.

There are, of course, always other options. A good deal of household waste may be incinerated or composted if you live in a rural area. Most people in these areas have a barrel for burning and whatever little is left over can be occasionally hauled off. The best plan is to reuse or repurpose anything you can.

Let your neighbors know if you are discarding something. They might need it. Wood and metal are generally kept for other new projects, or sent to a communal scrap yard so that someone else can use it.

Internet access can be available through satellite systems or cell phone hotspots. If your family must have a TV – many off-gridders do not – you can get satellite TV. Since you have access to the Internet, you will also be able to get Hulu and Netflix, too.

Always Look at the Big Picture

After you have weighed all the pros and cons of tiny house living, you'll find that the big picture shows that there are many possibilities when you want to build the right home for you or your family. It does require a huge commitment, but this lifestyle change can be quite fulfilling.

There isn't just one "right" way you can live off the grid. Tiny house building is not a competition, and no one cares if someone down the road has a tiny house that is more cleverly styled. The main thing is that you need to be comfortable wherever you are. Enjoying the adventure is the name of the game for off grid tiny housers.

Chapter 3 - Economics of Tiny Houses

The economy of a tiny house is one of the reasons why people find the idea so appealing. There are so many aspects of home building and home ownership that cost less if you are building a tiny house, as opposed to a conventional home.

Initial Cost

If you have built a home or worked with a developer in the past, it will be easier to compare the smaller costs associated with building a tiny house. From smaller lot size required to fewer materials and fewer hours of labor, you will find the costs much lower with tiny houses.

Many people ask tiny housers how much it costs to build a tiny house. As with any house, it depends on the type of materials being used, whether you use a professional builder or do it yourself with friends' help, and what fixtures you use. Lot size can vary a lot, too, depending on where you are building.

Suffice to say that the cost depends on many things, but it will almost always be substantially less than building a conventional home, unless you use high-end materials or find a very expensive lot on which to build.

The time involved also affects the total cost. If you have time to do the work yourself in your free time, your house will cost significantly less than if you are in a hurry and need to hire helpers to complete your house.

No Mortgage Interest – Short Term Loans

Many people save up money and pay cash for their tiny house. If you want to finance your tiny house, you probably won't qualify for a conventional mortgage. That doesn't mean you cannot get a loan, though – people get loans for mobile homes every day. Tiny houses are not much different. Whatever type of loan you get, the amount financed will be much smaller than a mortgage. If you are still living in a traditional house, you may be able to get a home equity loan to pay for your new tiny house.

How Do the New Tax Laws Affect Tiny House Buyers?

The new federal tax laws decrease the amount that the government will subsidize for interest payment on mortgages. This has raised questions about the best ways to borrow money for tiny homes, or refinance them, while still capitalizing on the lower rates.

If you just check out the new law, it appears as though the tax savings reductions in home mortgages may encourage homeowners to keep their debt as low as they can, and to sign up for loans with shorter terms.

The popularity of 15-year loans indicates that the attitude of consumers toward debt may be changing already. However, finance and tax specialists state that in most cases, a reward for paying off a mortgage more speedily is not so much financial as psychological.

Tax experts have argued that the new law should not make short-term mortgages so attractive to borrowers, because the tax savings for homebuyers are still substantial. The new tax laws allow you to deduct mortgage interest paid, but the option is worth less. Only three tax brackets fit into the 33% bracket. The old bracket covered 50% of top borrowers. So, even though many homeowners will experience lower tax bills, they may also have higher carrying costs on their mortgages. Tiny home buyers usually only have to finance an amount much smaller than people purchasing conventional homes, so they save money under the old and new tax laws alike.

Lawrence Kaplan, a partner with the Kenneth Leventhal Company, says that everyone has their own view on the new tax laws. He said he would not make any decision based solely on not saving as much on your taxes. The tax structure may well be changed before homebuyers see the end of their 15 or 30 year mortgage term. Many people who are not buying tiny houses are priced out of worrying about the new tax laws. To be able to afford a home, they must take out a long term, large loan. They won't have to do that if they purchase tiny homes.

Financial planners state that short-term loans can help a family save for retirement or collage. But they may be money ahead to have a smaller amount to finance, as is the case with people buying tiny houses.

When you do make mortgage payments, the principle is going into your equity, although this is not always the case with tiny houses. The money you save from borrowing less can be placed in a 401(k) or other plan, to earn money that is tax-deferred. You will have a great deal more disposable income and retirement monies if you are financing a tiny home.

If you plan to keep your existing house and are buying a tiny home for a vacation house that can be rented out when you're not using it, you can make money off your new house. In this way, the vacation house will save you money on your family trips, and make money for you the rest of the year.

Saving on Utilities, Including Going Off-Grid

When you buy a tiny house, you will reduce your needs for electricity. Even if you don't use any alterative methods like solar or wind power, your bills will still be substantially lower. This is because you will be heating and cooling a much smaller space. Your appliances may well be compact, too, which saves more on energy costs.

Many tiny houses are built or placed on lots outside the city limits, which means that you won't have to pay for water or sewage. You will have the initial expense of a well and a septic system, unless you use a composting toilet. However, once those are paid off, you won't have a water or sewage bill.

If you are like many tiny housers, your desire for a sustainable way of life, and your social conscience, will be in your mind even before you buy or build your tiny house. Find an appropriate lot that has access to sun and wind, if you plan to go off the grid. You can also make more immediate changes that will reduce your dependency on electricity.

Changing to Solar Power

The best way to get rid of your electric bills is by going solar or using wind power. Solar panels feed into batteries that you will use power from, to replace the electricity that you normally use. The size of solar panels you need will usually be somewhat smaller if you are just collecting passive energy for a tiny house. You can always upgrade to a larger system if yours does not give you enough electricity to run everything you would like it to.

The energy conserving appliances and solar powered lights you purchase for your home are suitable for use on the grid, as well. You can reduce carbon emissions while you save money on your electric bills. Even if you only have supplemental solar power when you first move into your tiny house, it will allow you to have lighting and some basic essentials in your home working, during storms or other times when the electrical supply to your home is disrupted.

Saving Money in the Winter

During the sunny months, there isn't an end to the free solar electricity usable during daylight hours. Your kids can play video games and you can watch TV. If you want to use more solar power than power from the grid, you'll want to turn off the power guzzling video game console and other appliances early enough in the evening that your batteries will have time to charge before dark.

This is totally different in the winter months, if you live in an area with defines winters, as opposed to Florida or California. You won't have the same luxury of using power until evening time, if you want to subsist mainly on solar power. Winter is not as forgiving when it comes to electrical demand. It does, however, bring its own benefits.

During the winter, there are other ways to save power. If you have a refrigerator that is designed for use with electricity or LP gas, it can even be turned off in the winter. Fit a large and covered area with a window opening, and use it like a refrigerator door in the winter. Place in this cupboard anything that needs to be kept cold, and set it in the area where your winter window is located.

There are some solar powered appliances, like torches and lights, that may receive enough light to charge up through a closed window, keeping out the cold but letting in the sunlight.

Appliances and Lights to Help You Live off the Grid

Your monthly electricity bill is influenced directly by how much electricity you are drawing from the grid. So, every appliance or light that you don't use the grid for will lower your electric bill.

The easiest place to look for immediate electrical savings is in your lighting. Hand-powered and solar-powered lights don't need power from the grid. You can charge them with electricity if you need to, though. Otherwise, you're saving money for the power they don't use. Rechargeable batteries are excellent backups for these types of lights.

Lighting Your Home Off the Grid

If you check your lighting solar panels in low light, you may note that they still charge even when not in full sunlight. The best lights with solar panels can last for years. Every tiny home should have a solar panel that comes with a longer lead to a battery pack, which then leads right to the two lights. You can turn these lights on or off, so they are usable as lighting for your desk, kitchen workspace or nightstand. Leave the solar panel in a window, so that it can gather sunlight whenever there is any, and the extra long leads extend to anywhere in that room where you might need them.

Newer units of this type have USB ports, so you can use them to charge iPhones, cameras, etc. It works quite well as a gift for teens who never remember to turn anything off when they leave the room.

Lower Property Taxes

Tiny housers are often asked building code questions. Tiny houses do not fit into the standard building codes of most communities. Many consider tiny houses as acts of rebellion. There are not very many municipalities that have any legal definition for tiny houses yet, so you may have to be "creative" in building one, or in finding a site. Once you establish your location, the property taxes will be similar to those assessed on modular homes, rather than conventional homes.

The owner of one tiny house building company, MiniMotives, was asked for her professional advice on building codes as they relate to tiny houses. Her name is Macy Miller. She is a tiny house builder and also works with her city. She states that the best place to learn about your local codes is your City Hall. Inside this government building, you'll find a planning department.

These planners are there to help builders of all types of houses to make sure that they are constructed to code. They must adhere to zoning regulations, as well. If you're speaking to someone in the planning department, make sure that you don't mention "wheels", even if you plan to build your tiny house on wheels. Then you would be transferred to the Department of Motor Vehicles, which is another whole problem. The problem there would be that the DMV will not be able to help you with building code questions.

Speaking with building code officials may not always help, but Ms. Miller still advises people to talk to them. This will help you and future tiny house builders, since planning departments will become more aware of tiny houses and the need to revise building codes.

If you go the way of some tiny housers and build or buy "under the radar", you may not have any taxes at all.

Saving on Materials

It's exciting to contemplate making that decision to build a home for you or your family. You may spend many hours designing it, revising various details, from light placement to counter space to bathroom size. You might spend months collecting materials, to ensure that you have whatever you need, before you start building.

Once you begin construction, you'll be pleased at the money saved on materials, as compared to conventional homes. You'll probably spend a lot of money, energy and time but the house will be a labor of love. After you have completed your house, you will be able to relax, and then the realization will hit you that you still have to set it up on your lot. This might include towing it on interstates and rural roads before you set it up on the lot you have chosen. It may not even be a permanent lot, which will save you even more money on taxes.

You can anticipate that people will ask you what the most difficult part of designing and building a tiny home is. It's a fair question to answer, because you may be able to entice others to join the tiny house movement. They won't commit the time unless they realize that they can overcome any challenges they might face. Your time spent in thought may be either about building or about moving your house. Most people who build their tiny homes in one place and then move them will find people with large enough trucks to make the move without a lot of money out of pocket.

Saving on Moving Costs

Some tiny house owners buy an inexpensive vehicle to tow their home to its new lot, although this is not always necessary. It's a good idea to build as close to your eventual site as you can, so that you won't have a long-distance haul when the house is complete. You can take vacation trips with your tiny house, and, as long as you can find RV parking, you'll usually have a place to park.

One Family's Story of Saving

Could you live in 300 square feet or less? What if you're sharing that small area with three other people? Tiny house families do it every day. When a family wants to save money and live free of a mortgage, they may buy a parcel of land and build a tiny house.

One family purchased land in the Blue Ridge Mountains and used materials bought from Craigslist to build a new tiny house for only $12,000. They enjoy a home that they do not owe any money on, which allows them to live off one person's salary and save the other's for vacations and other dreams. Their tiny house includes a sunny kitchen, a loft for sleeping and a lovely porch.

This particular tiny house has plenty of privacy, with separate lofts, and areas of the home dedicated to living, dining, eating, sleeping, and office working. They have a 12-gallon hot water heater, an apartment-designed range, a small refrigerator, a couch built in, a kitchen sink, a hand sink, a shower and a toilet. The full-light door and multiple windows bring in plenty of natural light and allow the family to feel like they live partially outdoors.

Why Did They Decide on Building a Tiny House?

Building a homestead that is mortgage-free fit into the family's long-term plan. After saving the money and buying the land, septic and well, they didn't have a lot of money left. They began building on a flatbed trailer, and since they were building tiny, it was fairly easy for them to find leftover, overstock and salvaged construction materials.

How Did They Keep Their Prices Down?

This family kept their costs down by using salvaged materials and handling all the labor themselves. They found on old trailer from a mobile home for a foundation. A neighbor donated the kitchen sink, since they were remodeling their conventional home. The oak used on the interior was salvaged from a local home that was being demolished. The refrigerator and lights were recycled from a closed restaurant. The materials for framing, along with the flooring, windows, stove and insulation were bought on Craigslist.

Do Families Feel Cramped in Their Tiny Houses?

On rainy, cold days, it may seem like tiny houses shrink. There is no option to go outside, so sometimes family members will feel cramped. They usually become accustomed to it after a year or two. Some tiny housers say that their key to not being cramped is to stay in the present and put everything away.

Advice for People Who Want to Live Small, Off-Grid

The first step for people who want to go off-grid and live small is committing to what will be a completely new lifestyle. Possessions must be pared down. Wardrobes must be, too. The tiny house should be designed around your regular activities. If you plan to cook all your meals at home, you'll need a larger garden and a full kitchen.

Avoid the temptation to compromise on facilities or fixtures. Organize your belongings and plan shelves that allow you to see everything on them. If you are married or have a family, practice asking for things you need respectfully. You may want to build a shed to store recreational gear and canned foods, and perhaps a washer and dryer.

    Be sure you have plenty of outdoor space for living. A big deck will work well in good weather. A covered deck will work in the rain, as well. Install a fire pit for winter evenings. Lastly, make sure that your whole family is committed to the new adventure, and always be clear about why you are living as you do.

Chapter 4 – Reasons why People Choose Tiny Houses

Tiny Homes are Eco-Friendly

Taking your life from a conventional home to a tiny home stops you from consuming as much from nature. If you go off-grid, you'll even be producing energy, instead of taking it away. Traditional homes require many resources to use and maintain. You can change that negative to a positive with a tiny house that sustains itself. Here are some reasons why people choose the tiny house lifestyle.

Reduce Your Energy Usage Right Away

Reducing what you consume is the first step in tiny house living. If you bring something into the house, it must be something that you need, and something that can be recycled when it is no longer needed.

Growing a Home

Instead of thinking about building a home, think about growing one. Green roofs, for instance, process CO_2, and they can even grow food for your home. They reduce your costs for heating and cooling.

Using Green Power

Of course, it does require resources and energy to produce your solar panels, wind turbines and geo-thermal taps. However, if you use them for going off-grid, you will offset the resources it took to produce them. Over the life of the products, you should make up the difference and extra.

Tiny Houses Save Money

There are many ways living in a tiny house can save you money. When you make the decision to build your tiny house, you likely will not need a mortgage to build it. If you do need financing, you can usually get a short-term loan, although they are somewhat hard to get, since tiny houses are still "new" to the banking systems.

Minimal Cooling and Heating Bills

Whatever you pay now for your utilities, you'll pay exponentially less – or nothing – for your heating and cooling bills in a tiny house. Even if you are on the grid, a tiny home will usually only cost between $10 and $35 per month for all your utilities.

Tiny Houses Are Inexpensive and Easy to Build

The cost for the materials needed for an average tiny house built on a trailer are about $20,000, if you buy everything new from a big box store. It can be considerably less if you buy off Craigslist or eBay. This doesn't include labor for any parts of building you are not comfortable doing yourself. There are tiny house workshops, too, if you want to learn to build the whole house yourself.

You Don't Need Your Own Land

Some people who build and live in tiny houses work something out with a landowner, rather than buying land. You may pay a minimal amount to rent the land, or perform a service like mowing or landscaping in exchange for the land you are using. You won't pay property taxes on land that you do not own.

No More High Mortgage Payments or Rent

If you live in a sizable city, you probably pay a substantial amount each month for rent or a mortgage payment. You certainly would not mind losing those payments. You can own a tiny house free and clear, sooner than you could ever own a conventional house.

Reclaimed Materials Allow You to Build Cheaply

Some people who have built tiny houses on trailers have done so for $3,500 or so. This is possible if you take time to find cheap or free reclaimed materials like siding, windows, wood and doors. If you have time to find the right materials, you can save a lot of money. You may also want to be open to design changes, since you may find cool pieces that you'd like to use in your tiny home.

Do Some of the Labor Yourself

You may not be comfortable with building, but if you attend workshops or have friends who can build, you can save a lot of money on skilled labor. Many tiny homebuilders do the rough work themselves, like carpentry, and hire experts for wiring and plumbing.

Save Money on Overpriced, Oversized Furniture

If you have a tiny house, you don't have room for much furniture. If you want to, you can choose expensive pieces, since you will only be buying a few. However, if you want to be a minimalist, you will get serviceable furnishings at good prices. You will probably include built-in closets, bookshelves and other storage space. This means no more purchasing whole rooms full of furniture.

You'll Have Lower Clothing Bills

Forget going to the store or online to buy all the newest styles of clothing, purses, shoes, etc. There will simply be no room for them in your tiny house. You can spend a bit more, to get clothes that you will wear longer.

Lower Maintenance and Repair Costs

When you own a tiny house, you deal with less. You will save on stress, money and time on repairs. Repainting a tiny house is a simple matter, and so is roofing. If you built or helped to build your house, you will have insight into how to do repairs easily.

The Tiny House Movement - Minimalism

It's amazing how many people will tell you they love their tiny houses. They are not much to look at, unless the designs were specially drawn. There are many reasons why you will probably be happier in a smaller house. Tiny houses are easier and quicker to clean. That has to be worth something.

Tiny Housers are Mentally Free

People love their possessions, and the more they own, the more they want to own. Rather than becoming hostage to your possessions, you can free your mind when you think less about "stuff" and more about the big picture.

Likewise, you will have more time to do hobbies or anything else you enjoy doing. You can pursue what really matters in life. Your family will be closer, and your tiny house will encourage your family to bond. You will interact with family members more and become more comfortable and familiar with each other.

Reconnecting with Nature

Many people prefer tiny houses because there are only a few spaces to sit and lots more time to spend outdoors. While tiny housers love their homes, they also enjoy exploring the world outside. A small home drives you outside. Without big screen TVs and gaming systems, you may be compelled to find relaxation outside the home, too.

Your tiny house will create a place that satisfies your needs, but allows you to move outside into nature. You can explore trails, wander prairies, stroll new streets and make new friends. These things will never be found if you spend your time sitting in your family room.

Tiny House Families Are Closer – Literally and Otherwise

For families with more than one child, a tiny house may seem even smaller than it is. The smallest of tiny houses are usually between 100 and 200 square feet. Even if you have a semi-large family, you can still live in a slightly larger version of a tiny house.

The Simple Life of Tiny Houses

Some people live in tents or their trucks or vans while they are building their tiny houses. You may make quick trips to the local grocery for food, and to the hardware store to pick up items you need for the house you and your family and friends are building. Until you're done with your house, you'll have to make trips to the Laundromat to do your clothes, too.

Lighting Use Outside Your Tiny House

To make the deck or porch of your home into an evening living area, install motion-detecting lights. If you have a path in front of your house, that can be lit, too. If you keep extra tools or recreational equipment in your shed, a light there will be handy, as well.

Staying Comfortable and Warm Off-Grid

Generating heat can be challenging when you live off the grid. It may sometimes be difficult to heat your whole tiny house with just solar panels and your deep cell batteries. You need to have a fuller strategy, which includes a slow-combustion fireplace or wood stove in the main living area and good insulation in the ceiling and walls. Proper window placement makes it easier to heat your house, as does passive heating, with large sized glass doors facing the positive sun direction. Trees will beautify your home site, but don't plant them so close that they block the sun.

One Man's Junk...

One of the best things about living a simple life is taking pleasure in what others might call junk. For example, who would need a hand operated pump in today's world? If you live off the grid, a pump like this will allow you to pull water from your well without power. How handy is that?

In the same way your techno-gadgets used to mean so much and now do not, many of the things you once thought were worthless have new purposes. Just like that hand-powered water pump. Solar-powered pumps make pumping easy in sunny weather. However, during cloudy days, instead of using a generator that needs fuel, the hand pump works quite well.

Nature Lovers in Tiny Houses Recycle Passionately

If you're a minimalist and you love the outdoors, you are much more driven to recycle anything you can. Living off the grid makes recycling more important than just helping nature and putting your recyclables in a separate container at the curb.

Now you will wonder what other purposes items may have, besides the one job they were intended to do. You can use egg cartons to start seeds, until you have hens and hence buy no more eggs. When you collect your own eggs every morning, you'll reuse those old egg cartons until they simply fall apart.

People throw out washing machines all the time. That is a huge amount of refuse to throw out. The drum from an old washer is perfect for building small outdoor fires. There are perforated holes for airflow, but they won't allow debris and embers to blow around. Since they are made from stainless steel, they are ideal for setting a barbecue grill on top.

Loving the Green Life

When you live next to nature, you can have a huge garden, or even add a greenhouse onto your shed, on the sunny side. Your neighbors will be happy to bring by old windows and doors you can use for your reclaimed greenhouse.

Using New Forms of "Currency"

Money doesn't always have the same value in a simple life. In addition, other things may have their own intrinsic value. Bartering was often done in years gone by, and it can still be done now. Your chili mix could be worth a couple of eggs. Herbs, especially if they are organic, will be popular with cooks who live nearby.

In the off-grid world, everyone checks in with their neighbors before they get rid of anything that may have potential value to someone else. Once a decision has been made to discard items like old, non-working appliances, friends are informed, in case they need any of the parts to repurpose.

Oven doors can be trash to one person and a treasure to another. If you're building a bunker for wildfire protection, an oven door survives extreme heat and has a window for viewing. It makes a perfect "window" for an underground fire bunker.

Gardeners Love Minimalist Living

Gardens are essential when you live off the grid. Nothing is quite as good at keeping vegetables and fruits fresh as leaving them where they grow until they are ripe and ready for harvest. When you look at home sites, look over the soil in the area. If you are able to grow organic vegetables and fruits, you'll have enough to feed your family and have enough left to barter with friends and neighbors. When planting your garden, include medicinal herbs, so that you can use natural treatments for injuries and illnesses. Many herbs have comparable effects to over the counter medications.

Check on the rainfall reliability in the area in which you are planting. You will need to be harvesting rainwater and collecting it in storage tanks, so you'll have something to use during periods that are dry. The larger your garden, the more rainwater you will need.

Networking with other Local Off-Grid Tiny Housers

When you go off the grid, you may find yourself living in a rural area. Not many city dwellers can live off the grid. Networking with the people in the rural area in which you choose to live will help you in identifying reliable local trades people, the stores with the best values and the people most qualified to help you when your solar system is in need of repair. When someone upgrades their system, they may be willing to sell you their old system.

Choosing the Best Building Alternatives

If you have acreage that is not restricted for tiny houses, you have the basis on which to build your home. You can clear the lot yourself, or have it graded for you. If you don't have a lot yet, you can build your home on a trailer bed.

A simple, tiny house still needs a sturdy roof and insulation. Wood stoves will allow you to use the abundance of dead wood in most forest areas to supplement your solar heating system. Living in a rustic way is something you may enjoy, although there will be times when you miss some of the old conveniences of home. Remember, you don't have a mortgage, and you only need a house for eating, sleeping and sitting. You can do all of these things, regardless of the size of your house. You can live with less and still feel blessed.

People who grew up on farms have a better perspective on the abilities they have for building and maintaining their tiny house. They are used to living in rural areas, so they will be more at ease right from the start.

Tiny House Essentials

Your tiny house or cabin will need plenty of windows to let in the light. A sleeping area, kitchen and living area will give you the room you want for your radio and laptop. Shelves are essential, for your food and supplies. Perhaps you will raise chickens, not just for eggs but also for meat.

Plan ahead so you that you have all your bases covered when you build. You can't just start building without plans, no matter how simple your house may be. If you're not a designer, it's quite easy to find many plans for all types of tiny houses online. You need the time to plan and the money or barter fodder to get the materials you need for building.

If you build a tiny house and your family grows, you can expand your tiny house or cabin. Adding a second story or expanding on the ground floor can be accomplished with the help of your neighbors.

Making the Transition to Tiny House Living

A tiny house can cost less than 1/7 the amount of a conventional single family home. It depends on your ability to find reclaimed materials and appliances. The tiny house movement is being called "dramatic downsizing" in the US. It is a pared-down lifestyle that allows you to gain economic freedom by minimizing expenses.

You may be surprised at how simply you can live. Many people are looking for a more modest lifestyle and less "stuff". Tiny houses are often defined as houses with 500 or less square feet, but many have 200 square feet or less. Some of these homes are built on trailers, due to old building codes, but they certainly do not have to be built on wheels. This isn't the main thing that draws people to tiny house living.

One tiny houser was tired of worrying about having a great credit rating (or not) every time he wanted to make a change in his life. His house runs on two solar panels and a car battery. He earns more than he spends now, which is quite a refreshing change.

The number of tiny houses in the United States is still, well... tiny. However, they are growing in popularity. The rate of conventional home ownership in the US has fallen to about 65%, which is its lowest point in nearly 20 years. Ironically, you can feel a lot freer in a small house, since you are living in a new and different way, and taking control of your life.

Tiny House Popularity

Tiny house for sale listings have greatly increased in volume in recent years. Tiny House Facebook sites have many followers and fans. Google trends have shown that the national interest in searching for tiny house information is higher than it has ever been. People who got in on the ground floor or the tiny house movement, some 15 or more years ago, notice the changes and are happy to welcome new members to the tiny house community. The need for plans and information for tiny houses is becoming increasingly larger.

Some tiny house advocates were once conventional homeowners, until the real estate bust in 2008. Following foreclosure, people are understandably hesitant to tie themselves up with mortgages again. Many tiny housers don't have any loans at all. They save money and use reclaimed materials with which to build their little houses.

More females aspire to the tiny house lifestyle than males, according to web traffic at the busiest tiny house websites. Whichever sex is doing more planning, tiny houses are not considered as strange as they once were. They are seen as "cute", and the cultural mores about living in tiny houses have changed.

In a survey of 2,600 US tiny house dwellers by The Tiny Life blog, it was found that almost 25% are between the ages of 31 And 40. Nearly 90% of tiny housers surveyed stated that they have at least some college level education, and over 60% had no credit card debt.

Tiny house plans are seen by some as the reincarnation of the original "Sears Roebuck house". Ready to assemble small house kits were sold by Sears between 1908 and 1940, and they sold almost 70,000 of the kits.

Some of the most tiny-friendly cities in the US include Seattle and Portland. They are open minded in their building code realism. Most tiny housers build or move their houses to rural areas, because many cities have outdated building codes into which tiny houses just don't fit.

Washington, D.C. sounds like an unusual place for tiny houses. But they are using space that was previously underutilized. It's called "infilling". A website shows off three tiny houses on one lot, where there used to be illegally parked cars. The new homeowners have a communal garden, outdoor oven, hot tub and fire pit. The site utilizes conventional electricity and incinerator toilets. The homeowners collect rainwater, which is moved by water pumps like those found in RVs.

Like many other areas, these homeowners cannot call their houses "permanent legal residences", due to old zoning restrictions. In order to get around these restrictions, the houses were built on wheels, so they are technically known as travel trailers. Codes exist mainly to maintain housing standards, and the director of Washington D.C.'s office of planning said she sees this little community as having high quality buildings and excellent environmental stewardship.

Addressing Building Codes

Cities need to control the types of homes that can be built within their area, to ensure that squatter camps are not set up. Officials in planning departments are trying to understand that different living arrangements will limit homelessness and give people homes they can afford. Where restrictions are eased, the way is paved for the legalization of tiny houses in the back yards of conventional homes.

In years past, the tiny house movement was small, and it flew under the radar of federal, local and state authorities. Many people wanted to build tiny houses, but were discouraged and gave up due to building codes and zoning issues.

It is believed that the demand for tiny houses will drive new legislation, and that laws will eventually change.

There is also the psychological hurdle that is placed in front of you, when you look at parting with many of your possessions in favor of a simpler life. Dramatic downsizing is too much for some people, but others find it liberating. It may take years before you are comfortable living with less.

Once people become accustomed to their tiny homes, they don't even feel claustrophobic. It helps that the houses are so efficient and cheap to heat and cool. Savings accounts grow and debts grow smaller, as people learn that they don't need everything they thought they did, in order to thrive. Your tiny house may just give you peace of mind that you never found anywhere else.

Conclusions

Tiny home living allows you to celebrate your achievements. The difficult times, financially and otherwise, are made easier when you remember that you are living without a mortgage, with a small carbon footprint. This was the goal that drove many tiny housers to build their houses in the first place.

Now and then, if you're feeling cramped, you can remind yourself that you have a couple lovely acres in a setting that appeals to you. Your well provides you with delicious, pure water. In addition, you don't owe anyone money.

Saving Carries Over to Other Aspects of Life

Trading your overpriced home for life in a tiny house will allow you to live more simply, and with fewer headaches. The lifestyle is much less stressful, and you will find out what disposable income is. Saving money for the future is a good motivator when you decide not to go out and buy things that you really don't need.

People who live in tiny houses are asked whether they have had to make any drastic life changes when they adopted the lifestyle of tiny house living. They say, instead that they now see all their old possessions as anchors, instead of things that define them. They start gardens and compost piles and even move in other family members.

Buying or renting land cheaply makes it easier to live off the grid, if that is one of your goals in tiny house living. Your house may be close to work, so that you are not putting a lot of miles on your car. Otherwise, you'll be defeating the purpose of living a simpler life and making your carbon footprint smaller.

Some tiny house owners choose to work from home, which is fine, as long as they have office space available in their homes. Tiny houses can always be added onto, if more space is needed.

Building and living in a tiny house, whether it's on or off the power grid, will change your life forever, and allow you to appreciate the important things in life, that have nothing to do with possessions. You will find yourself focusing on the things that mean the most to you and truly enjoying life more. So, what are you waiting for? Start your journey to the Tiny House lifestyle today!

*****

The Tiny House Lifestyle: Live More With Less

Introduction

Surely you have heard of the Tiny House Movement by now, haven't you? The movement is growing bigger each and every day and it seems that there is no way of stopping it! Basically, the Tiny House Movement is a social movement where people have decided to downsize their lives and the spaces that they reside in, and adopt the Tiny House lifestyle, both in theory and in practice.

Did you know that the typical American home is about 2600 square feet? Who needs that much space? By contrast, Tiny Houses are typically anywhere between 100-400 square feet. That's a pretty big difference! You should know that tiny houses do come in a variety of shapes, forms, and sizes, so by making the most of those spaces, they can feel much, much bigger. However, the main focus of every tiny house is simple living in a smaller space. Live better with less.

Every day, more and more people are joining this social movement for lots of different reasons. Some of the most popular reasons for moving into a tiny house are:

- Environmental
- Financial
- Emotional and Psychological
- Simply wanting to have more time and freedom to focus on the things that really matter

Most American families spend one-third to one-half of their income to pay for a roof over their heads. Think about that! How much money would you save every month, or every year, if you spent even half of that amount on housing only? This figure means that you will spend around 15 years of your working life just to pay for a roof over your head. Due to this problem, there are around seventy-six percent of Americans that struggle when it comes to finances, with many only being able to live paycheck to paycheck, never saving any meaningful amount of money, and not even getting to enjoy their home, because they are too busy working to pay for it!

The alternative to living this way is to move into a smaller space and get rid of the "junk" that clutters your life. Of course, we should keep in mind that tiny houses really aren't for everyone (though some would argue that you can find a tiny house to fit nearly ANY living situation!) Still, even if you can never imagine living in a tiny house, there are still some lessons to be learned from the Tiny House Movement and there are things that you can apply to your life to get out of the cycle of debt that around 70 percent of Americans are caught in.

Did you know that, on average, the typical single family home will cost you over $1 million over the course of thirty years? Let's take a look at these numbers:

You find a wonderful home that's perfect for your family - great. The purchase price is $290,000. That's not too bad, right? Well, let's say your down payment on that home will be $58,000 and then you will finance $232,000. You're still thinking that you're doing pretty good, right? The typical interest rate is around 6.41 percent, which will end up being $195,000 over the course of thirty years. You're now up to $485,000 for that home that was supposed to be $290,000.

Now, let's factor in the taxes and insurance over thirty years: that'll be another cool $180,000. Maintenance on your home will average you around $300 per month, so over thirty years that will come out to $108,000. What about major repairs? Over the course of thirty years, the major repairs to your home will cost you about $300,000.

Now, for your "perfect" home, you have now spent $1,073,000. Crazy! That puts a major dent in your finances. This is why families have such a hard time paying their bills and staying out of debt when they get in a home that is much too big for them and their needs.

So, what's the alternative? Well, let's read on to find out more about this social movement and why it has become so popular.

Benefits of a Smaller House

Many people have a very hard time getting their head around why anyone would want to live in a tiny house. Society tells us that "bigger is always better", which means that most people want a much bigger home, not a smaller one, and definitely not one that is less than 500 square feet! Like it or not, we judge our own success and that of others by the size of their home. However, the truth is that living in a tiny house has a lot of benefits – more than many people ever realize.

Following are ten advantages of living in a tiny house. These are just ten – there are many, many more. But these ten will get you thinking and start to show you a few of the many benefits that downsizing your life can have. If you're looking to simplify your life, reduce your expenses and stop having to live paycheck to paycheck, as well as your reduce your environmental footprint, a tiny house may be just what you need.

- A tiny house has a much lower initial cost. A tiny house is, obviously, smaller than a traditional one. This means that it requires less initial materials and labor. Since the size is so much smaller, the price to build or purchase one is a fraction of what a traditional house would cost. You'll save your wallet a big hit right from the very outset.

- A tiny house consumes much less energy. Due to the much smaller interior space, a tiny house requires less energy to heat or cool than a traditional house. Many of the tiny houses are actually on wheels so during the summer months, you can move it under a large tree to benefit from the shade and during the winter months, move it out into the sun to take advantage of daylight hours. Additionally, appliances in a tiny house are much smaller and therefore use less energy. With a tiny house, you can choose to live off the grid, using solar panels, compost toilets, wood stoves, and wind turbines. You'll be amazed how much money you save purely on energy and utilities every month. It all adds up very, very quickly.

- A tiny house uses less water and create less trash. In a tiny house, you have a much smaller hot water heater and shower, which means you'll be taking much shorter showers, saving water, and paying less in utilities. Additionally, if you choose to live in a tiny house, you're likely interested in creating less trash and reducing your ecological footprint. Both of these are beneficial for the environment and will save you lots of money. Good for you, good for the Earth – it's a win-win!

- A tiny house means lower maintenance costs all around. Think about it: replacing the roof on a 2,000 square foot house is going to cost you a lot more than you'd spend to replace the roof on a 300 square foot home, right? This is true due to the fact that the smaller size means less labor and materials. The reduction in maintenance costs applies to any and all repairs that need to be made. Over the course of even 5 or 10 years, imagine how much money you will save on repairs alone, and you'll see the benefits in living small.

- A tiny house means that you have less land to worry about and to maintain. Since the house is so small, you don't need a large piece of land (though some people love having land and all that comes with it – and a tiny house can easily fit into this lifestyle as well). It may be necessary for you to have land located outside the city, which means that the land is cheaper and the taxes are lower. Additionally, if your tiny house is located on a trailer, you will likely not have to deal with the annoying building restrictions and permits that are necessary to build a traditional home.

- A tiny house means you won't be shopping for household goods as much, which means that you'll have less clutter and more money in your wallet. After all, if you don't have anywhere to put something, you're not going to buy it, right? The only things you'll have in your tiny house are things that are absolutely necessary. Of course, that doesn't mean that your home won't be beautiful – it just means you'll save money by not buying things that you really don't need!

- A tiny house means you'll pay lower property taxes. The amount of property taxes you pay is tied to the value of your land and your home. Since both of these factors are much lower with a tiny house, the property tax bill will be much lower. The amount you're saving can be invested, saved for your retirement or to pay for your children's college, you can use it to go on vacation, or anything else you decide to do with it. More money in your pocket, less paid out in fees and taxes. Everyone likes that, right?

- A tiny house requires less home owner's insurance. This is something that can add up very quickly with a traditional home. Since tiny houses are generally considered less valuable, they are much cheaper to insure.

- A tiny house means you'll pay less interest. It's no secret that many times people have to borrow money to purchase or build a traditional house. When you borrow money, you end up paying interest. As you saw in the introduction, over thirty years, you end up paying almost as much, if not more, in interest charges than the actual value of the house itself. However, many times, people can pay cash for a tiny house, or can at least pay it off very quickly. This means you'll be saving a lot of money in the long-run.

- A tiny house means less stress. Overall, a tiny house is much easier to manage and to maintain. You'll have much more money and won't be struggling to balance and pay your bills each month. You may be living outside the city, or at least not in a cramped apartment or condo building, so you don't have to deal with all the noise and you can spend more time enjoying nature. Basically, living in a tiny home means life is much simpler and you're actually able to enjoy your life and family. And really, isn't that what it's all about?

Different Types of Tiny Houses

When it comes to tiny houses, there are a few different choices. Contrary to what you may see on TV or read on the Internet, tiny houses come in many different shapes and sizes.

The first is what most people would recognize as a Tiny House. This is, well, there's no simpler way of saying it, a "normal"-looking house…just smaller! I know, I know. But really, that's all it is and all it looks like. You can have one built on your property as a permanent structure or you can have it built on a trailer, so it is easy to move. If you do it this way, you don't even have to leave home when you decide to go on vacation! You can simply attach your home to your vehicle and go.

There are many companies springing up all over the world that specialize in building these types of Tiny Houses. Some will build on trailers only, and some will actually come to your land and build on a foundation or basement even. These companies often sell their extremely detailed blueprints, so that you can hire a local contractor if you want or, if you're really gung-ho, try to build it yourself! These traditional Tiny Houses come in all different shapes and styles, from Colonials to Craftsman, from A-frame cabins to Southwestern-styled Adobe abodes, and everything in between. Chances are, no matter your style preferences, you can find a tiny house builder or contractor or blueprint to match your dream home.

Another brand of Tiny House living has seen folks take pre-existing structures and convert them into tiny houses. These may not work for everyone but for certain situations, they are just perfect.

Some people have even gotten creative and converted old Airstream trailers and other RVs into their tiny home. Other people have even taken old school buses and converted them into a tiny house. You typically won't find blueprints for these types of conversions, since each project is so individual and unique. But if you're creative and handy, or know someone who is, a conversation project can be a really fun, inexpensive, and engrossing way to get your own tiny home.

One more option that is becoming more and more popular lately is a Yurt. These are circular, tent-like structures traditionally used by nomads in Central Asia that have really caught on with the tiny house movement lately. Their appeal lies in the fact that they are usually most less expensive than more traditional tiny houses, they require a lot less lumber and other expensive supplies to build, they can be more eco-friendly if you build them the right way, and many people find their circular structure and open space more aesthetically pleasing than the traditional outlines of a tiny house.

The type of tiny house you choose will depend a lot on your personal tastes and choices, as well as what you plan to do in your tiny house. If it is to be your year-round, all-the-time house, then a more traditional layout works quite well. If it is to be a vacation home or maybe an office space in your back yard, smaller options like an A-frame work really well. If traveling is your goal and you want to live and travel in style, then a bus or RV conversation project may be what you're looking for. The options are nearly as limitless as your dreams of what you want to do with your tiny house!

Whichever flavor of tiny house living you choose, the key is to create a house where you can save money, avoid clutter, and still live comfortably. The sky is the limit when it comes to choosing the type of tiny house you'd like to live in.

Design Tricks to Maximize Smaller Spaces

When you are living in a small space, such as a tiny house, it is necessary to do what you can to get the most out of the space that you have. People often cannot imagine how they could live in such a greatly reduced space. They feel they *need* to have a bigger house to live comfortably. They couldn't be more wrong! Following are some design tips to help you decorate and maximize your small space and to get the most out of living small.

When decorating your tiny home, one really important trick is to create "zones" in your tiny house. Consider the things that you do in particular spaces in your home: you work, you sleep, you eat, you relax. So in your tiny home, you can create separate zones for those particular activities. It doesn't need to be an entire wall or a completely separate room, like it would be in a traditional house. Making even subtle separations between these areas can help your tiny house to feel much larger.

Even without walls separating areas, you can still create "rooms" in your home. Use a large rug to designate the living room area. Use a different color scheme for the kitchen to visually separate it from the rest. Use mirrors in the bathroom or the sleeping loft to reflect the space and make it seem larger. Some people like to use curtain to temporarily separate an office space from the rest of the tiny house. The possibilities are endless – use what works best for you.

When choosing furniture, choose items that can be used for multiple purposes. For example, choose a table that you can use for your desk for working or paying bills, as well as used for a dinner table. Find daybeds or deep sofas that can be used for seating areas during the day and guest beds when you have guests over. You can find ottomans that can be an extra seat, a table, and even a secret storage area. Choose furniture elements that can be folded up or stacked to take up less room when you're not using them. Also, make sure that you put casters on your furniture so that you can move it around easily. When you're able, use wireless technology for your home/office gadgets, speakers, and lighting elements.

Trick your eyes into thinking the space is larger than it really is. You can do this by using floor to ceiling curtains, mirrors, and see through furnishings. Large windows on outer walls make the wall look bigger and truly open up an area. When the weather is good, have the doors or windows open. Many people find by building a porch area, they are able to extend their living space outdoors and greatly increase the size and openness of their tiny house. This also encourages children to get outside and play, as well as brightens up the entire space, lifting moods with it.

When decorating, choose larger pieces, but use fewer. Though you may think that this is counterintuitive, the truth is that using a few large pieces instead of several small pieces can make the room seem much larger. Every little nook and cranny doesn't need to be filled up with some piece of furniture that you'll never use. Your space will feel much larger if you only include items that you'll actually use. So, don't be scared of filing up the space that you have available with items that you'll use frequently. When a room is full of furniture that is put to good use, it actually seems to be larger than it really is.

Use soothing and even-toned colors instead of bright colors. Natural tones that mimic outdoor colors and land tones work really well. This will fool your eyes into believing that the room is much more spacious than it really is, as well as provide a soothing, natural feel to your place.

Of course, keeping all of the above in mind, you should customize your furnishings in your small space. When you customize the furnishings to meet your personal needs and desires, you're able to use all of your space and maximize the space that you have available. Don't rely on standard issued items or things that you used to have in your old living space. Take the opportunity to really craft your new tiny house living space to you as an individual or as a couple or family. The extra time spent on this will really help you feel at peace in your new place.

Splurge on your decorations in your tiny house, when possible. Use large pieces of artwork or a wall of bookshelves to deceive the eyes into believing that the space is larger. Also, a wall of bookshelves will give you space to display some of those knick-knacks and books that you have collected over the years, without having to get rid of them or having them clutter up every open space in your tiny house. Placing a mirror opposite of the bookshelf is another great way to open up the space and give the room a bigger feel.

Many times, that space between the tops of furniture and the ceilings is left unused. To maximize your space, consider using that area for displaying high-mounted or hanging elements. This will bring the eyes upward. For example, as in the above tip, consider taking your bookcases or cabinets all the way up to the ceiling. Use a beautiful chandelier or other large light fixture to draw the eyes upward, creating a sense of more space and utilizing all of the height of your tiny home.

Utilize the design element of sight lines. Tear down (or if you're building it yourself, leave out walls), install larger windows, use glass doors instead of solid ones in order to open up the views or connect spaces. On the other hand, you can use the design element of visual stumbling blocks, such as putting in walls or even screens to divide spaces and to force you to slowly take in the space, which will fool you and your guests into believing the space is much larger than it really is.

Remember to avoid the cluttered look. If you use up every little space, your home will feel much more cramped and small than it really is. You don't have to display everything you own. And you don't need to keep everything you had displayed in your old house. Keep those things that have importance to you and get rid of the excess. Group collections in specific areas of your home and allow them their own space. Then, since you don't have everything displayed all at once, you can change it out seasonally or according to your mood.

Even when you live in a tiny house, you can still have a very beautiful home, and make the most out of the space that you have. Many people wrongly assume that tiny homes are ugly, cold, or unwelcoming. This could not be further from the truth! Given the right design and using the above tricks and tips, you can make your tiny home just as welcoming and inviting, if not more so, than any large home out there. What's more, oftentimes, due to their cozy size, tiny homes actually feel much more warm and happy than larger, cold spaces. You'll be surprised how quickly your tiny home will feel like…well, home!

How to Eliminate Physical Clutter

You already know that, over the years, clutter tends to happen. No matter if you live in a house or an apartment, it's likely that you often feel the clutter all around you. We continuously buy stuff and never get rid of anything, so our homes end up full of junk and it can be quite stressful and overwhelming to think about clearing it out. However, no matter the size of the problem or mess, keep in mind that it can be done!

Before you can move into a smaller space, you're going to have to get rid of the junk and only keep what is truly important or necessary. So, start by spending just five minutes each day to sort through your clutter.

I know what you're thinking - five minutes of clearing will barely put a dent in that mountain of clutter in front of you. Don't think about the mountain; think about the first step. The important thing is that you're doing something about it. The best way to get started with anything is to take baby steps. As you begin to see that you're actually making progress, you will probably be more willing to spend more time each day at clearing out, and soon you'll have less junk getting in your way.

You'll see that by spending five minutes each day, pretty soon that first mountain will be cleared and eventually the entire closet. From there, the rest of the room. Eventually, the clutter will be cleared out of your entire home and you'll be well on your way to shrinking your living space and simplifying your life.

Following are some tips for clearing out that mountain of clutter:

In most cases, clutter begins due to papers. Typically, they end up in various stacks all over your house: in drawers, on the kitchen counter, on your desk - basically wherever you happen to lay them down. It's no wonder you can't put your hands on that power bill that came in last week – it's lost in a mountain of papers somewhere. To start the clean up: Choose a spot, one spot only, to designate for papers. When you get the mail, stop by the trashcan on your way in and immediately throw out the junk mail. Only keep what is important. Have a spot designated for receipts, warranties, and other things that must be filed away so that you can get your hands on them when necessary. You'll be surprised at how much this will do for that mountain of paperwork. You'll instantly rid yourself of junk papers and you'll know where every other important paper is.

Choose one area to clear out. Once cleared, it will be a "no clutter" zone. This can be the kitchen table, your desk, the kitchen counter, or even the couch. Wherever this location is, the rule will be "nothing allowed unless it's currently being used." Once you have designated this area, expand it until the whole house is that way. Of course, this will take plenty of discipline- but it can be done! When you choose a "no clutter" zone and being to clear it, take note of what was cluttering it up in the first place. If it's papers you don't need, get rid of it. If it's knick-knacks or decorations that you never use or look at, get rid of them. If it's toys or old furniture, you can donate them. If it's clothes, and you haven't worn it in the past six months, donate them too. You'll quickly find the items that you *really* use and the items that are just taking up space. These are the items that you need to get out of your life.

The ultimate goal is to clear off all of the flat spaces in your home, making them part of the "no clutter" zone movement. Of course, in your kitchen, you can have appliances such as the coffee maker, toaster, etc., but the clutter needs to be gone. For example, if the blender is still sitting there and you haven't used it in several weeks (or months) it needs to be put away. In the kitchen, start with one counter and work your way through each one. Now that your kitchen is a "no clutter" zone, move on to a shelf somewhere in your home. It can be a shelf on the bookcase or a shelf in the closet. Don't try to tackle the whole bookcase or the whole closet, just the ONE shelf. Throw out, or donate to charity, anything that is not essential. Pretty soon, that area will be neat and clutter free.

Look at your calendar and schedule a "de-cluttering" weekend. You may not feel like you can do a major clearing out right now, but make sure that you pencil it in for later in the month. This gives you plenty of time to prepare yourself and to recruit your family and friends to help you. The more hands on deck, the quicker this process will go and the easier it will be to make decisions on what should stay and what needs to go. Make sure you have boxes and trash bags ready. Make sure that you make some time to stop by to drop off donation items. You will probably not get your entire house done in one weekend, but at least it's progress, right?

When you're walking through a room, pick up five things and put them where they belong. If it's something that you're not using anymore, drop it in a bag or a box to donate. If the item is used often but doesn't really have a designated spot, take some time to select one and always make sure to return it to that spot when you're finished with it.

Stop and look around a room, thinking about exactly how you want it to look. Consider what furniture is necessary for the room and what doesn't belong but somehow ended up there. Once you've decided what belongs in the room and what doesn't, make an effort to get rid of what doesn't.

Sometimes, when you're sorting through a pile of clutter, you'll know exactly what you want to keep and what you want to get rid of. In some cases though, you'll come across an item that you don't exactly use, but you can't quite let go of it either. Have a "maybe" box for stuff like this. Put it there and then put a note on the calendar to go through the stuff again in six months and see how you feel about it then. In most cases, the answer will be to get rid of it because after all, you didn't touch it in those six months it was hidden away, did you?

Once you've gone through several piles of clutter, you will probably have a donation pile that's in the way. Put it in a box and put it in your car. Make it a point to take it to donate to charity the next day.

The biggest problem with decluttering is the clutter somehow always comes back because we always end up getting more junk.

This is where the discipline comes in. You can break the cycle of clutter by making a "30 Day List." This is a list where you jot down things that you really want, but aren't exactly a necessity. So write it down, along with the date. Then, don't buy anything except those essential things unless they have been on the list for at least thirty days. In most cases, the urge to purchase will be gone after that thirty-day mark. This will help you curb your impulse buys and you will prevent clutter and save money.

Enlist your kids, spouse, and/or roommates in the "declutter/no-clutter" lifestyle. Let them know that everything has a place and it would be nice if things were put in their place when they're not being used. This will help with keeping the house clean and free of clutter, as well as making sure that it's in the proper spot if someone else needs it. Of course, old habits die hard, so this isn't going to be an easy process, but lead by example. In other words, do what you're asking them to do and, pretty soon, it will catch on.

Paperwork tends to stack up because we don't really have a place to put it. Take a trip to your local office supply store and purchase some file folders. Label them and keep them in a file drawer. Make sure to keep extra folders and labels so that you can make new folders as needed. Once you have created a file system, use it on a regular basis. Sort through your piles of papers go through them quickly, throwing out or filing them. Never put anything back into the inbox or the pile.

Now that you've cleared out some of the paper and other clutter, take some time to go through your clothes, getting rid of the things that you never wear. Of course, you don't have to do this all at once, but when you're getting dressed to go somewhere, pull out a few things that you haven't worn in a while and either put them in a donate box or put them in a seasonal/storage box. Just choose a few things each time and eventually, you'll be rid of all the clothes that you never or rarely wear.

Pick a spot to store your medications if you don't already have one. Go through all of your medications and get rid of those that are expired. The key is to make sure you have only the bare essentials. If there are things you're allergic to, throw them out.

Take one of your drawers and dump it out. Sort everything into various piles: what belongs in the drawer, what belongs somewhere else, what should be thrown out/donated. Take some time to wipe the drawer out and then put back only what goes in it. Then, immediately deal with the other piles.

Learn to love your new uncluttered, simplified life. Make it the standard in your home. Eventually, you'll learn to hate the clutter. Once you've initially gotten the clutter under control, you'll be able to keep it that way. Living without clutter is essential to enjoying life in a tiny home, so the sooner you can de-clutter your life and learn to love living with less, the better off you'll be in the long run.

How to Eliminate Mental Clutter

Now that you have gotten the physical clutter under control, it's time to think about the mental/emotional clutter. You'll be surprised at how much it will help your mind to get the physical clutter under control, but still, life moves so quickly that the "noise" of stress, projects, worries, errands, and everything else can result in chaos in your mind. You may find that no matter what you do, you can't get a grip on the calmness you desire. Living in a tiny house will help with physical and mental clutter, so it's important to get a handle on both.

When it comes to physical clutter, you can go through it and throw out what isn't necessary. However, your brain is very complex and you can't simply go through the pile of thoughts in your head and throw out the bad and file away the good, right? So, what can you do to declutter and simplify your mind?

The truth is, decluttering your mind really isn't that difficult, when you stop and think about it. There are a few simple actions that you can take that will make a huge difference when combined. Look over the following tips and choose a few of them to see how much you can clear out your mind.

Firstly, and most importantly, don't forget to breathe. Sure, that sounds pretty easy, right? By simply taking the time to take a few deep breaths, and really concentrating on the process, you can begin to clear the clutter and noise from your mind. Some call it meditating, some call it peaceful breathing, some just call it relaxing. Whatever you call it, it's important to get in the habit of consciously doing it. So, next time you feel your mind beginning to stray, take some time to focus on the your breathing. Notice how the air flows into your body and then back out. This will chase the other thoughts out and all that you will be thinking about is your breath. Calmness will follow quickly from that simple exercise.

When your mind is going in a million different directions and you can't focus on just one thought, get a piece of paper and a pen and write each and every thought down. This will get them out of your mind and onto paper, so you won't forget them and you can take each thought one at a time. Some thoughts you will quickly realize are unimportant and they can stay on the paper. Writing down others will allow you to see their importance and you can deal with them accordingly. The important thing is to get them out of your mind and onto the paper, where you can more easily decide which ones to act on and which ones to let free.

Think about what is the most important thing in your life at the stage you're in now and what needs your focus the most. Take some time to make a short-list of these things- not everything that is on your mind should be there. Once you've done this, get rid of what is unnecessary. This will help to get rid of the pile of clutter in your mind.

If you like, you can keep a journal about your thoughts instead of simply writing them down in a list. Journaling goes much deeper and will help you to explore other facets that maybe you haven't consciously thought about. This may end up leading to some thoughts and things that you didn't even realize were taking up space in your mind. Once you've gotten them out, you can consider if it can be gotten rid of or if you need to explore the topic more.

In some cases, the clutter in your mind is due to the fact that you're not getting enough sleep or you don't have a very good sleep pattern. You may not need to change your sleep habits, but sometimes, that can make a big difference. Just consider making a few changes in your sleep habits - you may be surprised at how much sleep (or lack of it) impacts your mind.

Participating in some sort of physical activity can do a lot to clear your mind. Getting outside and exercising gets fresh air to your brain and gets rid of some of that pent up energy that is resulting in jumbled thoughts. You really don't even have to exercise - just get outside and enjoy nature, sunshine and fresh air. Listen to the rain. Try to get somewhere out of the city and all of the noise that comes along with it. Just being at peace with nature has been scientifically proven to lighten our moods and lift our energy. This will help you to calm down and will help you to be able to focus much better.

You may believe that watching TV is a relaxing, mindless activity. Nothing could be further from the truth on a mental level, however. Turning it off will do wonders for quieting your mind. Even "background" noise of television or radio will actually add to the noise in your head and cause your thoughts to become even more jumbled. What we think is a relaxing activity for us actually doesn't allow our brain to slow down and process things, thereby getting them out of the way and helping us feel more at peace.

Look at your "to-do" list and cut off half of it- you can come back to those things later if necessary, or you can delegate them for someone else to take care of. Take the things that are left on your list and choose the most important things to get done. By choosing to do less, you are able to clear the clutter in your mind.

Though it may seem a bit weird, by simply slowing down, you can more easily achieve a level of peace that you are looking for. Society tells us that we have to stay busy and move through things as quickly as possible. However, by making the conscious effort to physically slow down, you're telling the world that no matter what time constraints or demands are placed on you, you're not going to rush through your life. When you slow down physically, you're slowing down mentally and therefore clearing out the clutter. You're taking the time to focus on things that really matter, and letting your mind and body work at a more natural pace.

Anger and frustrations are a normal part of life, it's true. However, these emotions are truly not necessary, at least not to hang on to, or focus on, or let rule our thoughts and actions. Though this is definitely much easier said than done, you'll find that it's truly worth all the effort. You'll be so much happier and there will be less clutter in your mind. You must make the conscious choice and effort to not let things get to you.

Our society tells us that we must get as much done as we possibly can, which leads to multi-tasking. This leads to filling up your mind with lots of clutter and the result is you have nothing to show for your efforts. When you're multi-tasking, you're not as successful or productive as you may otherwise be. You should stop and put your focus on one thing at a time. Leave everything else alone until that one task is done. Then, move to the next.

If you find yourself becoming overwhelmed with thoughts and emotions, take some time to talk to someone. Sit down and talk to your spouse, your best friend, a family member, or even a professional. Sometimes, just getting all the junk off of your mind and saying it out loud is enough to free yourself of those burdens. When the time comes that someone close to you needs to vent, you can return the favor. You may be surprised to see how much of a difference it makes in your sanity by simply talking about whatever is on your mind.

The tiny house lifestyle can certainly help you live a more relaxed, focused, and genuine lifestyle. But to get to that point, you have to first be at peace with yourself. Simply changing environments won't do it for you. But if you approach the tiny house lifestyle with the right mindset, you'll find that you can really thrive, both emotionally and physically, in your new surroundings. And that's what it's all about!

Gardening and Other Pluses for a Tiny Backyard

When you live in a tiny home, you'll probably have a tiny yard as well. Many people think that by living in a tiny house, they will have no opportunities to get outside and do the activities that they really love, such as gardening. It's true; sometimes that having such a small space can make it quite difficult to garden. However, it is possible to have a cute, small patio garden, if you don't have land, or a regular, big ole' garden if you do have land. Designing your patio garden only requires that you have the desire to beautify your environment.

Of course, keep in mind that even small spaces require the very same design principles that are used for larger properties. No matter what the size or shape of your property, you can make the most of your yard. Following are some project suggestions and techniques that can help you to come up with some ideas to test out.

First of all, when you're getting started you must analyze your property. Make sure that you take note of the access to your property, it's shape, and it's surroundings. You also need to very carefully examine the sun exposure, the grade (slopes, etc.), and the quality of the soil of your property.

The first thing you must analyze is the access to your property. You may have a gate for your yard, or you may only be able to access your backyard by walking through your house and out the back door. You may only have a very narrow walkway to access your space. This will obviously make it much more challenging to bring in the necessary supplies to build patios, ponds, and other fun landscape elements. Therefore, access is a very critical part of designing your outdoor space. Before you can make a decision as to what you're putting in your space, you must know how you plan to get it there.

Secondly, you must consider the shape of your yard space. When it comes to standard subdivision lots, they are typically squared off, which creates a patchwork of box-shaped properties. However, a small yard is not necessarily square - they can be skinny, circular, oblong, or even pie-shaped. This means that you'll have to do a bit more planning to utilize the yard space that you have available. If you have a pie-shaped yard, you can hardscape most of it and create a nice garden at the tip. If you have an oblong piece of property, you can make it seem wider by contrasting it with circular items such as rounded plantings, a pond, and/or a patio. By using the design principle of contrast, you're able to trick the eyes.

Finally, you want to give some thought to how you plan to spend your outdoor time and dedicate your small yard to this purpose. You may choose to grow an herb garden, install a pond so you can relax, or even create a Zen garden for meditation. Once you've decided on a specific theme for your yard, you can put some thought into your landscaping, plant, and other materials. The best way to do this is to sit down with a pen and paper so that you can jot down your ideas- this helps to keep your thoughts from getting all jumbled up.

Following are some steps to decorating and maximizing your small yard.

Choose large pots for planting. When you use lots of smaller potted plants, it brings attention to the fact that you don't really have room for all those containers. However, when you choose large pots and combine several plantings into one, it makes the space seem larger. Also, keep in mind the odd rule: ones, threes, and so forth are much more interesting. So, plant several things in one large pot, or choose three pots of various sizes grouped together.

Bigger is better. When you have a large yard, breaking it up into smaller spaces makes it much more intimate. However, when you have a small space to start with, creating even smaller spaces does not promote intimacy, but claustrophobia. So, choose one large feature to be the focal point in your yard and build some interest around it. For instance, install a kidney bean shaped pond in a linear backyard and surround it with a patio to create room to entertain guests. Border your small property with some interesting layered foliage- greenery will blur your property line and make people think that the space is much larger than it really is.

Choose tall or climbing plants to draw the eyes upward. You can also build walls, install fencing or trellises, and use any of your property borders for planting. When you plant in the low or tight spaces, you draw attention downward, and you take up very valuable space that can be used for a pond, patio, or other fun feature.

Choose plants that are easy to maintain. If you choose plants that grow into a jungle, you'll be spending more time pruning than you will enjoying your area. The best look for a small yard is trim and tame. Choose slow growing plants that will fill in your flowerbed over time. Train your climbing plants to crawl up your walls or lattice-work and around statues and other elements. A topiary will add some shape and will look very refined.

Finally, blend your foliage- go beyond your property line and pay attention to foliage in the distance- try to incorporate plants that will blend into your background. For example, if there are trees beyond your property line, plant a tree on the edge of your property and that will blur the line between what belongs to you and what does not. Of course, this is an optical illusion, but it is very pleasing to look at.

Conclusion

The Tiny House Movement is becoming more and more popular with people of all ages and lifestyles. People are leaving their busy, noisy lives and settling for the quiet comfort and peace of a tiny house. They're ridding their lives of the clutter, both emotional and physical, and are learning to enjoy life instead of just living it. This is what the Tiny House Movement is all about.

The typical American home is around 2600 square feet and over the course of thirty years, which is the average mortgage term, will end up costing you over $1 million. That's not counting refinancing and taking out second and third mortgages to help pay for things. In fact, most Americans actually spend around one-third to one-half of their income just to pay for their house. This means that fifteen years of your working life are just to pay for the house that you're living in! That is no way to enjoy life. You'll be spending all of your time and energy to pay for the roof over your head, that you won't even get to enjoy it, much less any other area of life. Tiny Houses provide another way.

A tiny house is a fraction of the size- typically somewhere between 100 and 400 square feet. Tiny houses come in all kinds of shapes, forms, and sizes, but the focus is always the same: simple living in a smaller space. Enjoying life and your surroundings instead of breaking your back, and your mind, to try and afford it. Focusing on the things you love and need, instead of the things you want or the things that society says you "should" have.

Every single day, more and more people making the decision to move into a tiny house for various reasons, the most popular being:

    1)   Financial

    2)   Reducing their environmental footprint

    3)   Being able to have more time with family

The alternative to being in debt your entire life is getting rid of all of the junk that clutters your life, the physical and the mental, and moving into a smaller, quieter space. This will give you more time to spend enjoying your family. It will give you more time to enjoy a hobby or two. It will allow you to save money for retirement, for your children's college education, for a vacation, or pretty much anything else you decide you want to spend it on- instead of having to spend all of your money on bills.

Even if living in a Tiny House is not practical for you or your family at this point in your lives, you can take a few lessons away from this social movement and get yourself out of the cycle of debt that around seventy percent of American families are caught up in. You can learn to focus on the positive things in life. You can learn to stop and breathe and de-clutter your life. You can focus on *living. So*, even if you don't think that a tiny house is right for you and your family, you can still work to get rid of all the clutter you've built up over the years and clear out your mind so that you can focus on the things that are important.

The Tiny House Movement is showing no signs of stopping anytime soon. In fact, it has grown exponentially over the past few years. And all signs are that it will keep growing, as more and more people learn what the movement is all about. So if you want to simplify your life, save a ton of money, clear your mind and body, and focus on the things that are really important to you and your loved ones, then a Tiny House may be the perfect solution for you. What have you got to lose?

Good Luck, fellow Tiny House lovers!

*****

If you've enjoyed this collection, **please** consider leaving a review and letting others know what you thought!

Sign up for J.R.'s Mailing List to be notified of **New Releases** and **Special Sales**: http://eepurl.com/XxKR5

Made in the USA
Lexington, KY
17 April 2015